Ferdinand Gildersleeve, Portland Burying Ground Association

The Portland Burying Ground Association and its Cemetery

Ferdinand Gildersleeve, Portland Burying Ground Association

The Portland Burying Ground Association and its Cemetery

ISBN/EAN: 9783337191634

Printed in Europe, USA, Canada, Australia, Japan

Cover: Foto ©Andreas Hilbeck / pixelio.de

More available books at **www.hansebooks.com**

THE

PORTLAND

BURYING GROUND

ASSOCIATION

AND ITS

CEMETERY.

PORTLAND, CONN.:

MIDDLESEX COUNTY PRINTERY.

1897.

THE

PORTLAND

BURYING GROUND

ASSOCIATION

AND ITS

CEMETERY.

PORTLAND, CONN.:
MIDDLESEX COUNTY PRINTERY.
1897.

This book is compiled from the records, maps and papers of The Portland Burying Ground Association, with the exception of the names and time of service of the Sextons, which are given as herein indicated, no complete record having been kept.

The dates of the deaths of former officers were mostly obtained from monuments and gravestones.

It is hoped that it will prove interesting and useful to members and friends of the Association and to the general public.

F. G.

Gildersleeve, Conn., July, 1897.

These grounds are consecrated to a sacred purpose. They do not belong to the living. In the highest, the fullest, the noblest sense, they belong to God and to the dead. Consecrated and hallowed as thus they are may they thus remain. May they be kept inviolate: may they be free from desecrations forever.

—REV. FREDERICK J. GOODWIN, AT THE DEDI-
CATION OF INDIAN HILL CEMETERY,
MIDDLETOWN, CONN.

ORIGINAL OFFICERS

OF THE

Portland Burying Ground Association,

A. D. 1845-6.

President.

DAVID CORNWALL.

Directors.

ENOCH SAGE,

WILLIAM H. BARTLETT.

Treasurer,

DAVID WILLIAMS.

Clerk,

CHARLES L. SAGE.

OFFICERS FOR 1896=7=8.

President.

HOBART DAVIS.

Directors.

HENRY KILBY.

EDWARD S. HALE.

Clerk or Secretary.

FERDINAND GILDERSLEEVE.

Treasurer.

FERDINAND GILDERSLEEVE.

Superintendent.

HENRY KILBY.

Sexton.

JOHN STRICKLAND.

The Portland Burying Ground
Association

was formed by the Articles of Association found upon sub-
sequent pages and was organized at the first
meeting held, on Monday the 15th
day of December, A. D. 1845.

THE PORTLAND
Burying Ground Association.

ARTICLES OF ASSOCIATION.

The undersigned inhabitants of the town of Portland in the county of Middlesex do hereby associate for the purpose of procuring and establishing a burying ground or place of sepulchre adjoining the present burying ground near the dwelling house of widow Anna Strickland in said Portland.

ARTICLE I. Said Association shall be known and called by the name of "The Portland Burying Ground Association."

ARTICLE II. The officers of said Association shall consist of a President, two Directors, Treasurer, Clerk and such other officers as said Association shall direct.

ARTICLE III. The first meeting of said Association shall be called by Wm. H. Bartlett, on the 15th of December A. D. 1845, at six o'clock P. M. at the Methodist meeting house in said Portland by setting notices of said meeting on the school houses in Districts Nos. 1, 3, 4, and 5 in said Portland five days before said 15th of Dec., and when so met shall proceed to choose by ballot the officers provided for by the 2d Article aforesaid.

ARTICLE IV. Said Association shall have power to make from time to time such By-Laws as they shall deem proper for the regulation and government of said Association not inconsistent with the Laws of this State.

ARTICLE V. Said Association shall have power to raise the necessary funds to carry out the objects of said Association by a tax or otherwise as said Association shall direct.

Signed:

David Cornwall,
Amos Cornwall,
Andrew Cornwall,
David Williams.

Hatsel Penfield,
Alexander Hale,
Horace B. Buck,
Robert U. Richmond,

Seth J. Davis,
Sylvester Stocking,
Asahel Penfield,
Chester S. Hurlbut,
Brackett West,
Selden Cook,
John Ingraham,
Ralph Pelton,
Manson Hurlbut,
David Hurlbut,
Barnard B. Buck,
Joseph Goodrich, 2d,
Erasmus Gladwin,
Agift Pease,
S. Gildersleeve,
David Shepard,
Kellogg Strong,
Jeremiah Haling,
Chauncy Shepard,
Thomas J. Hubbard,
Jonathan Shepard,
Roswell Brooks,
Wm. H. Bartlett,
Wm. Lewis,
E. B. White,
S. C. Spalding,
Edward Lewis,
Jeremiah Button,
James Giddings,
Samuel Brown,
Egburt O. Button,
George Strickland,
Frederick Miller,
Alfred Payne,
Henry E. Cook,
Edward A. Penfield,
Hector Stewart,

Joel Strickland,
Joel Strickland, Jr.,
Charles L. Sage,
Enoch Sage,
Asa Strickland,
R. P. Norcott,
Daniel B. Strickland,
Erastus Strong,
Henry S. Conckling,
Wm. C. Lewis,
Elijah Norcott,
Erus Bell,
Sam'l S. Buckingham,
Samuel B. Reeve,
Wm. W. Campbell,
Stephen H. White,
Daniel Cheney,
George J. White,
Charles Dewolf,
George Bell,
Wm. C. Ranney,
Augustin Overton,
Wm. G. Savage,
Benjamin Abbey,
Abner Hall,
Hiram A. Penfield,
Horace Penfield,
Abel Penfield,
Alfred A. Payne,
Daniel Shepard, Jr.,
George M. Brown,
Elisha Brown,
William Pelton,
Moses F. Alexander,
Thomas Fessenden,
Wm. L. Dixon,
J. E. Goodrich,

Seymur Hurlbut,	Roswell Wells,
Ralph S. Stewart,	Isaac Stevens,
Russel Hopkins,	Henry H. Wells,
Russell Brainard,	Nelson Shepard,
Russel Penfield,	Edward Shepard,
Renselaer Rathbone,	David Crittenden,
David Sage,	Orren Hale,
H. E. Sage,	Horace B. Wilcox,
Alanson Strickland,	John Reeves,
Jonathan Wetherill,	Job H. Payne.

CERTIFICATE OF SECRETARY OF STATE.

STATE OF CONNECTICUT ss

(Office of Secretary of State,
(Hartford, Aug. 22, 1848.

I hereby certify that the articles of Association of "The Portland Burying Ground Association" are on file in this office; and as appears from the endorsement thereupon were received 19th December, 1845, by Daniel P. Tyler, then Secretary of State.

Attest,

J. H. TRUMBULL, *Clerk,*

for JOHN B. ROBERTSON, *Secy. of State.*

TOWN CLERK'S CERTIFICATE.

Recd. Dec. 15, 1845, and registered in Lib. 3, page 164, in the records of Portland.

Test. SYLVESTER STOCKING   *Register.*

Names Signed on the Original Articles of Association after the Record was made upon the Town of Portland Records.

Evelyn White,	John C. Russel,
Chester Goodrich,	Edmund Hubbard.

James A. Hale,
David Hale,
Levantia Overton,
Nelson Pelton,
Turner Moulton,
Ralph Northam,
Lucius P. Stewart,
Philip H. Sellew,
Asher N. Rowley,
Sam'l C. Spalding,
Charles Ames,
Noah Shepard,
Hervey Talcott,

Francis Hale,
Sarah Hale,
Mrs. Elizabeth Buck,
Francis A. Pelton,
Noah B. Strickland,
Mrs. Betsey Stewart,
Chauncey Taylor,
Joseph Coles,
Hezekiah G. Pelton,
Joseph Williams,
J. L. Thompson,
Wm. S. White.

NAMES SIGNED TO ARTICLES OF ASSOCIATION IN RECORD BOOK.

Elizur Goodrich, Jr.,
Luther Wilcox,
Elijah Colton,
Nancy Shepard,
Alfred C. Penfield,
Amial Strickland,
Sanford Stewart,
Chester Brown,
John I. Worthington,
Mrs. Rebecca R. Arthur,
George W. Bell,
Sally Ward,
Elizur Abby,
Lucy Brainerd,

Edwin G. Dunham,
Mrs. Anna Strickland,
Henry Gildersleeve,
Hobart Davis,
F. Gildersleeve,
Chas. H. White,
John R. Ames,
Geo. W. Concklin,
John Strickland,
Joseph C. Gladwin,
Oliver Gildersleeve,
Henry Gildersleeve, Jr.,
Henry Kilby.

GILDERSLEEVE, CONN., Feb. 22, 1896.

HON. SECRETARY OF STATE, Hartford, Conn.

Dear Sir:—The Articles of Association of The Portland Burying Ground Association are on file in your office as appears from the Ctf. thereto attached of which enclosed is a copy. They are also recorded upon the Portland Town Records.

I understand that this makes it a legal corporation. If not will you kindly inform me what further action is necessary to give full corporate powers to sue, and be sued, give deeds of burial lots, etc.

Yours truly,

F. GILDERSLEEVE.

STATE OF CONNECTICUT,

SECRETARY'S OFFICE.

Hartford, Feb. 24, 1896.

F. GILDERSLEEVE, Esq.

Dear Sir:—I do not understand that anything more is required to make The Portland Burying Ground Association a corporation under Connecticut law.

I assume that a certified copy of your original certificate of organization would be received in court as evidence of the corporate existence of the Association.

Yours truly,

W. C. MOWRY, Sec'y.

R. S. H.

BY-LAWS AND REGULATIONS

As amended and adopted October 13th. A. D. 1894.

SECTION 1. The annual meeting of the Association shall be held on the second Saturday of September in each year at such time and place as shall be designated by the managers. In the event of a failure to hold the annual meeting on the second Saturday of September all officers will hold over and their acts shall be lawful until others are elected in their stead.

SEC. 2. Notices of annual and special meetings of the members shall be signed by the President or Clerk and be given by posting a copy upon the public signpost and advertising in a newspaper published in Middlesex County and in such other ways as deemed best by the Board of Managers, at least five days previous to such meetings, and meetings shall be called upon written request to the Managers by not less than five members.

SEC. 3. Notices of meetings of Directors and Managers shall be given by mailing a written notice to each Manager at least five days before such meetings, or in any other manner in the discretion of the Board of Managers, such notice to be signed by the President or Clerk.

SEC. 4. The President shall preside at all meetings of the Association and at all meetings of the Directors, of which board he shall be a member *ex-officio*; and in his absence the senior Director or such other person as the meeting shall direct.

SEC. 5. The President, Clerk. Treasurer and Directors shall constitute a Board of Managers to manage the concerns of the Association and make a report of their doings at the annual meeting of the Association.

SEC. 6. The Treasurer shall have charge of all the moneys of the Association and shall pay out the same under the direction of the Board of Managers. He shall annually, or oftener if required, present a report to the Board of Managers.

SEC. 7. The Clerk shall keep a faithful record of all the acts and proceedings of the Association and also of the Board of Managers and perform such other functions incident to his office.

SEC. 8. There shall be a Superintendent of the Cemetery appointed by the Managers who shall have the general direction and control under the Board of Managers of the grounds and all improvements thereon. Also of all property belonging to the Association and keep an account of the same.

Sec. 9. There shall be a Sexton or Sextons appointed by the Board of Managers who shall be an assistant to and under the direction of the Superintendent.

Sec. 10. All graves shall be opened by the Sexton or some person approved by the Superintendent and no interment or disinterment will be allowed without a written permit from the Superintendent.

Sec. 11. The Superintendent shall be allowed a reasonable compensation for time spent in laying out lots and the placing of monuments, grave marks and other stones and for any other service rendered for the benefit of the Association. He shall render his account to the Treasurer for whom special services were performed and the Treasurer shall collect pay for the same.

Sec. 12. No hedges, stone or brick wall or any kind of wooden enclosure of lots or graves will be allowed. If any enclosures are allowed to go to decay and ruin so as to be unsightly and in the judgment of the Managers a blemish upon the grounds they must either be put in order or removed by the lot owner or by the Superintendent at the expense of the lot owner after due notice.

Sec. 13. No owner, agent or guardian of a lot or lots will be permitted to raise the earth, form terraces or to place or set any foundation, monument, head or foot stones or corner stones except it be done under the supervision of the Superintendent.

Sec. 14. Owners of lots or those having charge of them will not be allowed to leave heaps of earth or rubbish of any kind on or about their own or the lots of others or in the Cemetery. If so left it will be removed by the Superintendent at the expense of the lot owner.

Sec. 15. Proprietors of lots may plant and cultivate shrubs and plants upon their lots under the advice and control of the Superintendent, but as they are often neglected the Association reserves to themselves the right to remove, at any and all times, any tree, shrub or plant that is in any way objectionable and in case of failure of the owners to remove them after due notice they will be removed at the expense of the lot owner.

SEC. 16.   All graves must be covered to a level with the ground in the lot, or if a single grave not in a lot, to a level with the surrounding ground.   No mounds to exceed four inches in height to be made over graves; after grave marks are placed the grave to be leveled.   When a grave sinks or caves in it must be filled to a level with the adjacent ground and all graves so kept at the expense of the lot owner or friends of person interred therein.   Graves sinking below the level of surrounding ground within six months after filling shall be refilled by the Sexton without pay.

SEC. 17.   It is desirable that a permanent grave mark be placed at each grave with a suitable inscription thereon, the mark to be of some durable material subject to the approval of the Superintendent.

SEC. 18.   It shall be the duty of proprietors of lots to place and keep in repair permanent mere-stones or land marks at the corners of their lots under the direction of the Superintendent. No corner stone or mark and no enclosure, monument or grave mark shall encroach upon the public drives or pathways.

SEC. 19.   All persons employed in the construction of vaults, tombs, erection of monuments or grave marks or work of any kind will be subject to the control and direction of the Superintendent. Any person failing to conform to this rule will not be permitted to work in the Cemetery.

SEC. 20.   Vaults or tombs, monuments and grave marks shall be of durable material subject to the approval of the Superintendent.

SEC. 21.   In the prosecution of any work in the Cemetery a place will be designated by the Superintendent for the deposit of all refuse material and rubbish which shall not remain longer on the grounds than is actually necessary for the finishing of the work and the work shall be forwarded without unnecessary delay.

SEC. 22.   No person shall have use of or title to a lot or grave nor hold it by selection against other purchasers until the same is paid for at the price set by the Managers.

SEC. 23.   In each case of interment or disinterment a statement giving the name, date of birth and death, residence, and if possible place of nativity and such remarks as may be desired to be placed on record of the person to be interred or disinterred must be given to the Superintendent and recorded by him in a book kept for that purpose. Whenever interments or disinterments are to be made at least one day's previous notice thereof shall be given to the Superintendent and a permit obtained therefor.

SEC. 24. Drivers of carriages must remain on their seats or stand by their horses during funeral services. No horse or team of any kind shall be left in the grounds unhitched. And any creature found running at large in the grounds will be impounded and the owner held for any damage.

SEC. 25. The Superintendent is fully empowered as special constable to arrest all who violate any reasonable rule of the Association or State Law touching Cemeteries.

SEC. 26. The interment of the remains of any stranger or poor person not otherwise provided for may be at such place as the Managers direct and the Superintendent shall record the names of such person and their place of burial with such other remarks as may be desired and are obtainable and a properly inscribed grave mark should be placed at such grave.

SEC. 27. Lots may be assigned and transferred from one owner to another provided the consent of the Managers is first obtained and such transfer giving the names of the parties be recorded upon the record books of the Association. Transfers without such consent and record will not be valid.

SEC. 28. All deeds of lots, conveyances and contracts shall each be signed by the President and Clerk, who are hereby created the agents of the Association for this purpose and such instruments shall be registered by the Clerk before delivery.

SEC. 29.   The Clerk shall keep a register or record of all sales and transfers of lots for burial purposes within the grounds of the Cemetery which shall show the number of both lot and section and size of the lot, the name of the purchaser, the price paid, the date of sale and such other matters as the Managers shall require. A map or maps of the Cemetery property showing accurately the location and size of each lot shall always remain in the office of each, the Clerk and Superintendent, and at such other places as may be fixed upon by the Managers

SEC. 30.   All deeds of lots must be recorded upon the record book of the Association and the title does not vest until such record is made.

SEC. 31.   Any person may become a member of the Association by signing the articles and becomes a member by owning a lot with deed properly recorded.   Each member is entitled to one vote at all meetings of the Association.

SEC. 32.   Not less than five members shall constitute a quorum at any meeting of the Association, and two Managers and the Clerk a quorum at any meeting of the Managers.

SEC. 33.   The Managers may at any time fill any vacancy which may occur among the officers or in their own number.

SEC. 34.   This Association will accept donations and bequests from any person and the Treasurer or any other officer of the Association is authorized to receive the same.   The gift or bequest may be on condition that certain lots or graves are properly cared for.

SEC. 35.   The President and senior Director shall be with the Treasurer a committee to have charge of donations and bequests to the Association, the Association to accept the same by vote.

SEC. 36.   The Clerk shall report to the Registrar of the town the names of the Superintendent and Sexton in charge of the Cemetery and any change thereafter immediately after appointment or change.   (Sec. 110, Statutes 1888.)

SEC. 37.   The seal of the Association shall contain the words "The Portland Burying Ground Association, Portland, Conn., 1845" and shall be used by the Clerk or such other persons as the Managers direct.

SEC. 38. There shall be a Secretary of the Association chosen by ballot at the same time the other officers are chosen, whose duties and powers shall be those usually incident to that office. The Secretary and Clerk may be one and the same person and may be voted for on the same ballot. The words Clerk and Secretary may be synonymous terms for the same officer at the pleasure of the Association.

SEC. 39. These by-laws and regulations may be altered and amended and repealed at any annual or special meeting of the Association, the purpose of so doing being specified in the call.

SEC. 40. All by-laws, rules and regulations heretofore adopted that conflict with the foregoing are hereby repealed.

The members of the Association, their families and friends and the public shall be allowed at all times access to the grounds, observing the by-laws and regulations adopted. all gates and other entrances to be closed when leaving the Cemetery at night.

As it is the object of these by-laws and regulations and the earnest desire of the officers and managers of this Association to make and keep this last earthly resting place of our beloved dead in as sacred, beautiful and becoming a condition as possible, it is requested that every person co-operate with the Managers in every possible way "To accomplish this consummation most devoutly to be wished."

FORM OF DEED.

No.   **BE IT KNOWN THAT**   &.

The Portland Burying Ground Association

Of the Town of Portland, County of Middlesex, and State of Connecticut,

In consideration of........................Dollars, received from
....do give, grant,
bargain, sell, and confirm unto the said........................
....
LOT No........................SECTION No..............
in the Burying Ground of said Association, situated in said Town of
Portland, said........................feet long in a Northerly
and Southerly direction, and........................feet wide in
an Easterly and Westerly direction, and contains..............
........square feet.

To HAVE AND to HOLD to h and h heirs and assigns forever as
a burial place for the dead, and for no other purpose whatever, subject to the Articles of Association and the By-Laws, Rules and
Regulations of said Association now existing, and such as may
hereafter be adopted. It is expressly agreed that the said lot shall
not be transferred without the consent of the Board of Managers,
certified upon the instrument of transfer, by the clerk of said
Association.

Witness the Corporate seal of said Association, and the
signatures of its President and Clerk this.... ......day of.....
......A. D.,

THE PORTLAND BURYING GROUND ASSOCIATION.

President.

Clerk.

Signed, Sealed and Delivered in the Presence of

....

STATE OF CONNECTICUT,)
                                              } ss.
COUNTY OF MIDDLESEX.)
                  PORTLAND,......   A. D.,
Personally appeared..............   ...President,
and. ....   .Clerk of the
Portland Burying Ground Association, and acknowledged the
same to be their free act and deed.

Before me,..................   .Notary Public.

The Managers have had printed for sending out the following circular :

"The attention of the managers has often been called to the condition of lots and graves which were wholly neglected. In many cases these lots and graves belong to families once prominent in our town who have left no kin to care for them.

As the income from the general fund can be used to good advantage in beautifying and caring for the whole cemetery, the surest way to provide against an individual lot or grave being neglected and to have it kept as neat and beautiful as possible for all time, is to give or leave a sum of money to the Association as a permanent fund on the condition that the income, only, be used by the Association to keep such lot or grave, and the monuments and grave marks thereon, in good condition.

Families often become extinct, move away, have so many cares or other good reasons that it is impossible to give the needed attention to these matters. But an Association of this kind never dies or becomes extinct, and money set apart or left in this way insures permanent care of a lot and graves.

There are so many advantages in the money being given in one's life time, in addition to the satisfaction of seeing the work done, that it is needless to call attention to them.

The income from One Hundred Dollars safely invested would be sufficient to take good care of the lawn of one lot. To include the cleaning and care of monuments and grave marks would require income from a larger sum. A less sum would yield enough to care for a single grave.

Any officer of the Association will be glad to give any information on this subject.

Inclosed is a form of gift or bequest."

FORM OF GIFT OR BEQUEST.

I hereby give and bequeath to THE PORTLAND BURYING GROUND ASSOCIATION, of Portland, Connecticut,.................Dollars to be and remain a permanent fund, the income only therefrom to be used by said Association to keep Lot No......Section No...

or the graves of .... in the cemetery of said
Association in good condition and to do whatever is necessary to
keep clean, repair, preserve and renew any tomb, monument or grave
mark thereon.

[If this special fund is set apart during lifetime erase the words "and bequeath," if
a bequest in a will, leave it as it is.]

Whenever any lot or grave is neglected the Managers usually call the owner's attention to it by sending
the following circular :

"Your lot in the cemetery needs putting in better condition.
Please give it your early attention.

It is desirable that our cemetery should be made and kept as
beautiful as possible, and we ask you to aid us by promptly attend-
ing to the above request."

HISTORY OF THE CEMETERY.

The land now occupied by and under the control of The Portland Burying Ground Association and enclosed within the present stone wall was obtained in the following manner. The first purchase was one and one-half acres more or less adjoining the old burying ground on the South, being the north side of the Cheney lot, so called. This purchase was from Mrs. Anna Strickland and her warranty deed is dated February 9th, A. D. 1846. It is to The Portland Burying Ground Association and the consideration was one hundred and fifty dollars. This deed was recorded March 16, 1846, in the Portland Land Records, in Volume 1, page 301. The land was laid out in lots with provision for single graves.

The next and largest addition of land to the cemetery was by gift from Mr. Sylvester Gildersleeve. It contains five acres and is the present southerly part. Mr. Gildersleeve gave, in 1860, six hundred dollars for its purchase of the Strickland sisters. The warranty deed is dated October 29, A. D. 1861, and is from the four sisters Asenath, Martha, Amy and Vienna Strickland, and is made direct to The Portland Burying Ground Association. It was recorded October 29, 1861, in the Portland Land Records in Volume 7, page 427.

This land is laid out in sections of four lots each as shown on the map of both the Strickland purchase and the Gildersleeve gift, made by Mr. Joseph C Gladwin, October 1, A. D 1894

The older and northerly part of the cemetery was conveyed by warranty deed dated January 24, A. D. 1767, "in the 7th year of the reign of our Sovereign Lord George the Third of Great Britain, etc. King" by William Bartlit, of Middletown, in the county of Hartford and Colony of Connecticut in New England to Capt. Jeremiah Goodrich, Capt. David Sage and David Robinson, a committee for the third Society in said Middletown. The consideration was five pounds and five shillings lawful money. The deed specifies that it was sold to the "committee as aforesaid for the use of the third Society in sd Middletown for a publick burying place for said Society wherein to bury their dead, to the said committee for the publick use as aforesaid, and to their successors in said office, their heirs and assigns forever, one certain piece of land lying on the East side of Connecticut river in said Middletown containing one acre and a half of land lying at a place commonly called the Plains and being part of that land which was lately called Indian land and is butted on highway both northerly and easterly and on my own other lands both westerly and southerly, which acre and one-half of land shall be laid out beginning at the northeast corner of the land which I lately bought at the Vandue of the Indian land and to extend westward by the highway about eleven rods and from thence about southward sixteen rods and from thence easterly to run such a point as may measure one acre and a half of land and by butting as aforesaid."

This deed was acknowledged before Joseph White, Justice of the Peace, and was witnessed by Joseph White and Eben'r White, and is recorded in Chatham Land Records, Volume 1, page 79, by Jonathan Penfield, Registrar, January ye 2d, 1769.

In 1862 The First Ecclesiastical Society in Portland, by Horace B. Wilcox, Franklin Payne and G. C. H. Gilbert, their committee thereunto duly authorized, for the consideration of one dollar and other good causes and considerations, devised and leased to The Portland Burying Ground Association their interest in the burying ground last mentioned situated near and adjoining ground of the said association, containing two acres more or less.

This lease was dated April 7th, A. D. 1862, and recorded April 8, 1862, in Volume 6, page 220, of Portland Land Records.

These three documents conveyed all the land now enclosed by the present stone wall and is all under the control and care of The Portland Burying Ground Association.

From the dates cut on some of the grave stones it would seem that there had been several interments on the Bartlit land before he deeded it to the Third Society's committee in 1767. Many if not all of the stones bearing much earlier dates were removed here with the remains of the persons from the burying ground which was formerly between the lands of the Middlesex Quarry Company, and Brainerd Quarry Company.

Among the earliest interments were Nathaniel White and his wife Mary. She died first, on Jan. 31, 1767, and his death followed eleven days later on February 11th of the same year.

Richard Goodrich, who died March 11th, A. D. 1767.

Rev. Moses Bartlit, died Dec. 27, 1766, aged 58, for 34 years pastor in this place.

Rev. Cyprian Strong, D. D., died Nov. 17, 1811, in the 68th year of his age, for 44 years minister here.

Rev. Hervey Talcott, died Dec. 19, 1865, aged 75 years, in the 50th year of his ministry here.

The length of continuous service in the ministry of the First Congregational Church in this place by these three pastors, was upwards of one-hundred twenty-eight years and they all rest in this cemetery. Such length of ministerial service in one church is rare in these days.

The cemetery is most favorably situated. The views from the southern and highest portion are extended and fine, embracing the Connecticut River and its green meadows with the surrounding hills which bound a beautiful section of country.

The soil being of a dry sandy nature is especially suitable for the purpose. Every effort has recently been made to improve and beautify the grounds. Many of the gravestones in the older portion have been righted and cleaned and water introduced through pipes from a well on neighboring land to a brownstone fountain in the newer part.

While the larger cities have given much attention to and expended large sums of money upon their cemeteries, making many of those sacred places beautiful and attractive, there is no reason why we should not also use the advantages nature has given us to make our rural city of the dead equally beautiful. There is plenty of evidence upon all sides that greater interest is being taken in these matters than formerly. Cemeteries are receiving more attention and the monuments and grave marks are kept cleaner and in better condition.

Thousands of dollars have been and will continue as time goes on to be expended upon monuments and lots in our cemetery and they should not be neglected.

There is no better indication of good taste and high Christian civilization than solemn respect for the memory of the honored dead and that can not be better shown than by keeping attractive and beautiful the lots and graves in the cemetery where they sleep.

ORGANIZATION AND HISTORY OF THE DOINGS OF THE OFFICERS.

The first meeting of the Association was held as provided in the Articles of Association on Monday, the 15th day of December, A. D. 1845, at the Methodist Meeting House (on Rose Hill) and officers were chosen.

At an adjourned meeting held on the next Monday evening, December 22, A. D. 1845, at the same place the original By-laws were adopted. At the second annual meeting held Monday, January 9. A. D. 1846, it was voted to purchase one and a half acres of land. The committee appointed to report a plan consisted of Ebenezer B. White, Asher N. Rowley and David Cornwall. This committee reported to the adjourned meeting held January 12, A. D., 1846, and it was voted to "purchase of Mrs. Anna Strickland land adjoining the old burying ground sufficient to lay out a burying ground on the plan reported." This is the land mentioned in the history of the cemetery. All persons interested were invited "to meet with teams and implements for the purpose of grading the ground without charge to the association, such invitation to be given in the several schools or in such other way as the managers think proper."

At the same meeting a plan was voted for the selection and assigning of lots after the ground had been graded and fenced, suitable provision was made "for a place of burial of the remains of any stranger or poor person not otherwise provided for," and the clerk was to record the name and age (if known) of such person and the place of their burial." It was at this meeting that a stone wall was decided upon as the most permanent and in the end least expensive manner of enclosing the grounds.

The managers reported to the annual meeting held January 1, A. D. 1849, the "laying out of the grounds into new lots according to the plan of single lots" and the records show to whom lots were assigned and certificates given under the plan adopted.

At the annual meeting held at the house of S. Stocking, on

January 2, 1854, the By-laws were by vote altered and amended
to provide for the officers holding over till others were elected, in
case annual meetings were not regularly held.

The next annual meeting for election of officers etc., was
held at the store of S. Gildersleeve & Son, January 6th, A. D. 1860,
and adjourned to the Center Church on Monday the 13th January,
and again adjourned to January 27th, and again to February 10th,
all in 1860. At this meeting the following votes were passed.

"Voted, That this meeting manifest a sense of esteem and grati-
tude to Mr. Sylvester Gildersleeve for his very liberal donation of
$600 to pay for the addition of five acres of land to their burying
ground and their wishes that he may long live to enjoy the pleasure
inseparable from acts of munificence conferring equal benefits on
the present and future generations."

And at this meeting it was voted that this land be enclosed
with the "present" yard by a stone wall and graded and laid out in
sections of four family lots each, the manner of numbering of the
sections and lots, the disposal and giving deeds, the prices of lots
and single burial places, the settlement of accounts of all persons
contributing to the improvement of the grounds, were all discussed
and voted upon.

At the annual meeting held on January 5th, 1869, David Cornwall, Esq., who had been the Association's President since the organization in 1846, tendered his resignation, and Mr. Seth J. Davis
was elected President.

At an adjourned meeting held at the Center Church, Monday,
January 25th, 1869, a tax of five dollars on each lot was voted, for
fencing and improving the grounds.

With the money realized from this tax the stone wall was completed and the grounds very much improved. It was also voted to
arrange for lots with members who had contributed labor, to deposit in Savings Banks the money received from sale of lots, and to
restrict interments in the old ground without written consent of
one or more of the board of managers.

At a meeting held January 14, 1873, it was voted that the managers be instructed to arrange with a collector for the collection of
the tax of five dollars on each lot.

At an annual meeting held at the store of S. Gildersleeve & Sons, on Thursday, October 19. A. D. 1893, it was

Voted, That the cemetery be surveyed at as early a day as possible and the sections marked by boundstones.

Voted, That Hobart Davis. Henry Kilby, John Strickland and Joseph C. Gladwin be a committee to procure such survey and boundstones and a plat of the cemetery.

The Secretary and Treasurer was also authorized to procure suitable books for the correct keeping of the records and accounts of the Association. And a committee was appointed on amending the By-laws and Regulations.

At the annual meeting held on Saturday, October 13, 1894, the present amended By-laws and Regulations were adopted and voted to be printed with such other matter as is of interest and worthy of being put in permanent form. the clerk to procure such printing. It was also

Voted, That the clerk procure a seal and that it should contain the words "The Portland Burying Ground Association, Portland, Conn., 1845." and it shall be the corporate seal of the association.

Voted, That the new form of deed of lots as read at this meeting be adopted.

Other votes were passed about having printed notices to owners of lots to have them put in order, also to furnish all members who desire printed copies of the By-laws and Regulations.

At the meeting held September 14, A. D. 1895. Mr. Joseph C. Gladwin reported that he had completed three maps of the cemetery, one of which is lodged with the President, one with the Secretary and one with the Superintendent.

At the annual meeting held on Saturday, September 12, A. D. 1896, Mr. Henry Kilby. the Superintendent, reported that he had successfully introduced water through pipes from a well on Mr. Alexander Hale's land into a brownstone fountain in the cemetery.

LOT OWNERS ON STRICKLAND PURCHASE.

Names.	Lot No.	Names.	Lot No.
Taylor, Chauncey,	81	White, George J.,	52
Taylor, David,	122	Warner, Orren, Jr., (part),	62
V		White, Ebenezer B.,	64
Valentine, Chauncey,	89	Williams, David,	69
W		Wetherell, Jonathan,	91
Wheeler, Charles and		Vacant in June, 1897:	
William,	6		16
Ward, William and Salley,	27		77
White, James W.,	46		119
White, Evelyn,	50		120
White, Stephen H.,	51		121

LOT OWNERS ON GILDERSLEEVE GIFT.

Names.	Sec. Lot	Names.	Sec. Lot
A		**D**	
Alexander, Lucy,	12—4	Dickinson, Ira,	3—3
Ackley, Elijah,	15—3	Day, Isaac H.,	18—4
Ames, Mrs. Elizabeth,	40—3	Davis, Hobart and Sarah M.,	
" " "	40—4		22—3
Ackley, J. Franklin,	52—2	Davis, Hobart,	22—4
B		**E**	
Bell, Eros	2—3	Edwards, Watson,	59—4
Brooks, David W. (s. part)	11—1	**F**	
Brown, Earl, (part).	15—2	Fountain for water,	14—3
Buck, James F.,	16—3	**G**	
Buck, Elizabeth,	16—4	Gleason, William H.,	1—3
Button, Daniel,	17—1	Goodrich, Chester.	3—4
Brainerd, Olia N.		" Charles C.,	18—1
Bolton, George W.	20—3	Frederick W.,	18—2
Buck, Henrietta L.	32—4	" John Q.,	23—4
C		Gildersleeve, Henry Jr.,	32—1
Crittenden, Daniel,	1—2	" Ferdinand,	58—1
Cornwall, David,	4—1	" "	2
" "	4—2	" "	3
" "	4—3	" "	4
" William,	4—4	**H**	
Clark, John H.,	6—4	Hale, Oliver M.,	6—1
Crittenden, Charles G.		Hale, James A.,	7—1
(w. part),	20—1	Hale, David,	7—2
Cornwall, A. Nelson,	21—1	Hale, Francis,	7—3
Cornwall, Andrew,	21—2	Hale, David,	7—4
Cornwall, Charles F.,	21—3	Hale, Fred'k A.,	A—2
Cornwall, Harvey B.,	21—4	Hurlburt, Simeon P.,	11—4
Case, Monroe H.,	31—1	Hopkins, Russell (part),	12—2
Cox, George and Isaac,	31—3	Hurlburt, Alanson,	13—1
" " "	31—4	Hurlburt, David,	13—3
Concklin, George W.,	50—1		

Names.	Sec.	Lot.	Names.	Sec.	Lot.
W			Wells, George W.,		19—4
Wilcox, Horace B.,		3—1	White, Wm. Starr,		31—2
.. ..		3—2	White, Charles H.,		39—1
Wilson, William,		13—2	.. ..		39—2
White, Edward E.,		19—1	**X**		
Wells, Roswell,		19—2	**Y**		
Wells, Henry H.,		19—3	**Z**		

NUMBER OF BURIALS FROM 1869 TO SEPT. 1, 1897
INCLUSIVE.

Number of Burials by John Strickland, Sexton, in the Cemetery of The Portland Burying Ground Association.

Year.	Date of first Burial.	No.	Year.	Date of first Burial	No.
1869,	Feb. 3d,	17	1884,	Jan. 12th,	17
1870,	Jan. 5th,	27	1885,	Jan. 14th,	20
1871,	Jan. 10th,	22	1886,	Jan. 14th,	19
1872,	Jan. 11th,	14	1887,	Jan. 6th,	17
1873,	Jan. 22d,	15	1888,	Jan. 22d,	18
1874,	Mar. 15th,	23	1889,	Jan. 1st,	18
1875,	Jan. 17th,	18	1890,	Feb. 24th,	14
1876,	Jan. 26th,	14	1891,	Feb.	15
1877,	Jan. 5th,	22	1892,	Jan. 9th,	18
1878,	Jan. 11th,	15	1893,	Mar. 20th,	†12
1879,	Jan. 24th,	19	1894,	Jan. 10th,	19
1880,	Jan. 7th,	20	1895,	Jan. 2d,	19
1881,	Feb. 1st,	*28	1896,	Jan. 2d,	19
1882,	Mar. 3d,	16	1897,	Feb. 2d,	11
1883,	Jan. 6th,	19			

Total, 525.
*Largest No.
†Smallest No.
Oct. 25th, 1871.   "Believed to be the last time the old Hearse was used."

LIST OF OFFICERS. PAST AND PRESENT.

PRESIDENTS.

1. David Cornwall,   ·   ·   ·   1845-1868
   Died May 3, 1874.
2. Seth J. Davis,   ·   ·   ·   ·   ·   1869-1877
   Died August 11, 1877.
3. Evelyn White,   ·   ·   ·   ·   ·   1878-1886
   Died October 16, 1886.
4. Henry Gildersleeve,   ·   ·   ·   1893-1894
   Died April 9, 1894.
5. Hobart Davis,   ·   ·   ·   ·   1894

DIRECTORS.

William H. Bartlett, ·   ·   ·   ·   ·   1845-1859
     Died August 8, 1894.

Enoch Sage, ·   ·   ·   ·   ·   ·   1845-1848

Asher N. Rowley, ·   ·   ·   ·   1849-1859
     Died Dec. 29, 1868.

Seth J. Davis, ·   ·   ·   ·   ·   1860-1868
     Elected President Jan. 5, 1869.

Philip H. Sellew,   ·   ·   ·   ·   1860-1868
     Died Jan. 18, 1873.

Evelyn White, ·   ·   ·   ·   1860-1878
     President in 1878.

Henry Gildersleeve, ·   ·   ·   1869-1893
     Elected President October 19, 1893

Hobart Davis, ·   ·   ·   ·   1878-1894
     Elected President October 13, 1894.

Henry Kilby, ·   ·   ·   1893

Joseph C. Gladwin ·   ·   ·   1894-1896
     Died September 1, 1896.

Edward S. Hale, ·   ·   ·   1896

TREASURERS.

David Williams,   -   -   -   -   -   -   -   1845-1860
                    Died August 12, 1863.
Ferdinand Gildersleeve, -   -   -   -   -   1860

CLERK OR SECRETARY.

Charles L. Sage,   -   -   -   -   -   1845-1848
                    Died August 9, 1864.
Enoch Sage,   -   -   -   -   -   -   -   1849-1893
            Resigned on account of failing eyesight.
Ferdinand Gildersleeve, -   -   -   -   1893

SUPERINTENDENT.

Henry Kilby,   -   -   -   -   -   1894

SEXTONS.

1. Seth Strickland.
2. Ammial Strickland. Began July 19, 1828. Finished March
27, 1837; these dates given by his son, John, the present Sexton.
3. John Shepard.
4. George Strickland. With the exception of Ammial Strickland
no dates could be obtained, and this record was given from memory
by old residents.
5 John Strickland, the present Sexton, was appointed January
25, 1869, and has held the office continuously since.

LIST OF NAMES OF PERSONS BURIED IN THE CEME-
TERY (KNOWN AS THE CENTER CEMETERY) OF
THE PORTLAND BURYING GROUND ASSO-
CIATION, OF PORTLAND, CONNECTI-
CUT, ENDING WITH DECEM-
BER 31, A. D., 1897.

This list was obtained from inscriptions on monuments and gravestones, from records of the sextons, Seth Strickland and John Strickland,* and from information received from individuals and other available sources. Every effort has been made to have it correct and complete.

The managers had the following notice advertised for six days in the *Tribune* and the *Penny Press*, daily newspapers published in Middletown, that all might have opportunity to give information and to correct errors:

SPECIAL NOTICE.

The Portland Burying Ground Association are about to publish in a book, a list of the dead lying in the Center Cemetery, Portland. To make the list as complete as possible, all persons are requested to give the names of deceased friends and others, with date of, and age at death, whose graves in this cemetery are not marked by headstones or monuments, with inscriptions, the names to be forwarded at once to Henry Killey, Superintendent, Gildersleeve, Ct.

F. GILDERSLEEVE, Clerk.

Gildersleeve Ct., Sept. 2, 1897.

After the list had been prepared and in manuscript the following notice was also published in the *Middletown Tribune*, and substantially the same in the *Penny Press:*—

CENTER CEMETERY.

A LIST OF DEAD ARRANGED TO BE PRINTED.

The managers of the Portland Burying Ground Association have had prepared a list of the names of the dead lying in the cemetery in Portland known as the Center Cemetery. This list is now at the Middlesex County Printery, about to be set in

* If the other sextons kept records they could not be found.

type and printed, and all persons are invited to call there and examine it for the purpose of giving additional information and correcting any errors. This list is to be published in the Cemetery Book and as it will be of interest to the public it is very desirable that the list be complete and correct before it is put into permanent printed form.

While no pains have been spared to have this list correct and complete, there are, undoubtedly, remains of persons buried in this cemetery without grave marks or records of any kind.

As the records of burials have been imperfectly kept, if kept at all. the managers have been unable to ascertain the names of such persons.

LIST OF THOSE BURIED IN THIS CEMETERY.

A

Name of Deceased.	Years.	Months.	Days.	Date of Death.
Abbey, Sophronia,	21			July 10, 1837
Emily,	31	—	—	Oct. 13, 1848
Frank R.,	2	—	-	Sept. 2, 1854
Elizur,	—	-	—	Jan. 9, 1892
Ambrose,	—		-	Feb. 14, 1881
Harmony,	45	-	—	Oct. 18, 1833
Thomas,	72	-	-	Mch. 24, 1824
Samuel,	80		—	Aug. 10, 1806
Henry A.,	4		16	Nov. 25, 1820
Asaph,	55			Dec. 17, 1831
Benjamin,	-	—	—	July 31, 1792
Lois,	64		-	Sept. 29, 1825
Elizur,	3	6		May 3, 1838
Elizur,	76		—	June 29, 1856
Betsey,	80	5	24	Oct. 17, 1863
Benjamin,	55			Apr. 11, 1865
Henry E.,	13		-	Feb. 13, 1861
Mary G.,	-	13	—	Sept. 7, 1855
Mary E.,	32			July 26, 1854
Emily,		3		Nov. 17, 1851
William,	—	- -	—	July 3, 1858
Sarah,	-			Mch. 21, 1812
Gerard,		—		May 18, 1825
Ackley, H. Ruth,	80	—		Jan. 11, 1885
William F.,	-	4	15	April 11, 1858
Alice E.,	—	6	14	Oct. 2, 1870
Henrietta,	- -	—		Feb. 5, 1875
Akins, Samuel,	71			June 25, 1804
Mary,	26	—		Mch. 31, 1766
Sarah,	—	—	—	Jan. 16, 1808
Roard,	—	—	—	Oct. 27, 1795
Robert,	49	—	—	Oct. 27, 1795
Alexander, Moses F.,	52	—	—	June 1, 1870
Gurney H.,	-	—	—	Jan. 28, 1892
Harry P.,	—	—	—	Jan. 15, 1892
Daniel S.,	-	10	11	Sept. 11, 1844
Alden, Harry P.,	—	—	—	Dec. 22, 1891
Charlotte A. W.,	34	4	7	Oct. 19, 1885
Harry Percival,	19	2	20	Dec. 22, 1891
Alin, David,	—	—		Nov. 18, 1790
Ames, Abigail,	6	—	—	Feb. 8, 1777
Theodosia,	63	—	—	Nov. 21, 1807

Name of Deceased.	Years.	Age at Death. Months.	Days.	Date of Death.		
Ames, John R.,	76	—	—	June	10,	1872
Vienna,	30	—	—	Jan.	23,	1799
John,	—	—	2	Jan.	10,	1799
Charles,	76	—	—	Aug.	26,	1881
Catherine C. L.,	84	—	—	Oct.	15,	1892
John,	56	—	—	Oct.	29,	1824
Vienna P.,	30	—	—	Jan.	28,	1799
Henry,	44	—	—	Oct.	10,	1847
Nicholas,	72	—	—	Dec.	3,	1817
Frederick L.,	42	—	—	Oct.	17,	1876
C. Walter,	21	—	—	June	19,	1886
Abigail R.,	19	—	—	June	18,	1769
Abigail,	19	—	—	June	18,	1769

Whole No. A's, 55.

B

Bates, Samuel,			4	Feb.	8,	1781
Job,	74			Aug.	15,	1795
Samuel,	21		—	Jan.	30,	1777
Sarah,	83			Jan.	16,	1784
Alsey,	—	8		Feb.	9,	1787
Babbitt, Elijah,		13		Nov.	28,	1790
Baker, Vienna A.,	26		—	Jan.	26,	1852
Vienna,	11					
Bakster, Rebecca,			—	Jan.	30,	1812
Baley, Viney,			17	Oct.	13,	1776
Betey,	3			Jan.	27,	1799
Phinehas,	4		—	Aug.	9,	1776
Bailey, Sophia,	64	—	—	Dec.	20,	1879
Mary,	60		—	Nov.	2,	1801
Abraham,	59			Apr.	23,	1810
Barbit, John,	—	—	—	Aug.		1799
Bartlett, Mrs. Dr.,	—		—	Oct.	23,	1826
John,	—	—	—	Aug.	29,	1800
Thomas,	—		—	Feb.	10,	1811
Bartlitt, Elihu,		—	12	May	11,	1774
Moses, (Rev.),	58	—		Dec.	27,	1766
Moses, (Dr.),	71	—	—	Mch.	3,	1810
Margery,	33	—	—	Apr.	24,	1775
Bartlett, Wm. H.,	79		—	Aug.	8,	1894
Mary E.,	11	—		Apr.	28,	1880
Julia,	77	—	—	Nov.	8,	1846
Joel,	58	—	—	Apr.	3,	1822
Samuel,	53	—	—	Mch.	5,	1834
Dency,	64	—	—	Feb.	10,	1845
Eunice W.,	47	—	—	Aug.	24,	1867

Name of Deceased.	Age at Death.			Date of Death.		
	Years.	Months.	Days.			
Betsey W.,	83	—	—	Apr.		1873
Cornelia L.,	37	--		Mch.	16,	1859
Rosalia L.,	16	7	—	Apr.	13,	1856
Alfred H.,	2	3	—	Aug.	28,	1871
Abel,	—	—	—			
Hulda,	—	—	—			
Mrs.,	—	—	—	Sept.	21,	1836
Bartwit, Joseph,	—	—	—	Feb.	1,	1810
Barnabee, Chandler,	61	—	—	Apr.	16,	1860
Mary,	70	—	—	May	19,	1862
Beach, Rev. A. C.,	75	—	—	July	30,	1881
Jane T.,	75	—	—	Mch.	9,	1895
Laura M.,	15	—	—	Sept.	28,	1873
Beebe, Mary R.,	65	—	—	Jan.	6,	1820
Mary,	—	—				
Molly,	2	—	—	Nov.	9,	1790
Alfred,	4	—	—	Oct.	8,	1790
Bell, Chas.,	31	—		Aug.	3,	1838
Eros,	64	—		Apr.	20,	1867
Cynthia,	30	—	—	Oct.	25,	1846
Emma A.,	—	10	—	May	25,	1845
William,	—	—	—	Feb.	21,	1887
Mary H.,	—	—		Jan.	2,	1896
George,	74			Feb.	11,	1857
Anna,	84	—	—	Aug.	30,	1869
Beldin, Sally,	—	—		Oct.	11,	1813
Bement, Kezia,	87	—		May	5,	1843
Elizabeth,	90	—		Sept.	29,	1848
Anna,	55	—		Jan.	25,	1848
Mrs.,	—	—		Mch.	22,	1815
Bidwell, Anna,	—	10		Nov.	2,	1779
John,	15	—	—	Nov.	2,	1795
Eunice,	3	—	—	Apr.	5,	1782
Agnes,	9	—	—	Oct.	23,	1776
Josiah,	31	—	—	Aug.	23,	1790
Annar,	25	—	—	Feb.	5,	1777
Sarah,	—	—	2	Feb.	4,	1777
Daniel,	73	—	—	Feb.	28,	1791
Sally,	52	—	—	Feb.	21,	1837
Bliss, John P.,	37	—	—	Aug.	18,	1840
Clorinda,	53	—	—	Apr.	21,	1859
John,	—	—	—			
Abby Ann,	—	—	—			
Boardman, Seth,	1	9	—	June	15,	1777
Elizabeth,	2	5	—	Aug.	1,	1770
Howel,	6	—	—	Aug.	26,	1775
Samuel,	20	—	—	Jan.	12,	1777

Name of Deceased.	Age at Death.			Date of Death.
	Years.	Months.	Days.	
Boardman, Samuel,	50	—	—	Apr. 13, 1787
Bolton, Geo. W.,	67	—	—	June 2, 1876
Martha E.,	53	—	—	Nov. 30, 1871
Bosworth, Elizabeth,	22		—	Apr. 28, 1775
Bowe, Lucy,	69	—	—	Sept. 15, 1851
Bowers, Prudence,	—	—	—	Dec. 10, 1859
Samuel,		—	—	Oct. 1825
Mrs. C.,		—	—	Mch. 20, 1812
Mrs.,		-	-	Feb. 15, 1819
Mrs.,		—	—	Feb. 20, 1800
Brainard, Sarah L.,	62	—		Aug. 25, 1893
Brainerd, Emily M. P.,	81	—	-	June 17, 1887
Emily M.,	72	—	—	Jan. 3, 1883
Brewer, Mrs.,		—		Aug. 27, 1798
Mrs.,		-	-	July 16, 1805
Brooks, Percy G.,		—	21	Aug. 6, 1896
John A.,			—	Apr. 4, 1893
Mary,		9		Dec. 28, 1816
Mary,	36		—	Apr. 29, 1821
Sybil,	41	—		Mch. 7, 1839
Roswell,			-	Mch. 20, 1857
Wm.,		—	—	May 20, 1829
Brown, Dorcas,	78		—	Apr. 3, 1812
Nathaniel,	92	—		Mch. 22, 1826
Sarah,	94	—	—	Aug. 21, 1841
Mrs. N.,		—		Aug. 28, 1822
Jonathan,	78			Mch. 9, 1826
Chester,	46	—		Mch. 31, 1858
Sarah,	94		-	Aug. 21, 1841
Caroline F. D.,	77	—	—	June 21, 1888
Chas. S.,	15	6	—	Mch. 16, 1857
Chester G.,	—	15	7	Apr. 19, 1848
Geo. M.,	37		—	Sept. 23, 1850
Elisha,	84		—	Nov. 24, 1854
Esther,	78		—	May 16, 1853
Josephine A.,	27	—	—	Sept. 14, 1860
Martha M.,	13	—	—	Oct. 22, 1852
Mary A.,	16	—	—	Dec. 1, 1852
Wm. A.,	9	7	—	Mch. 31, 1848
Frances E.,	6	—	19	Apr. 19, 1843
Frederick Wm.,	17	—	-	Nov. 11, 1848
Esther M.,	4	—	-	Dec. 6, 1833
Samuel F.,	—	1	—	Jan. 9, 1849
Ida,	—	—	—	Jan. 14, 1886
Chas.,	—	—	-	Oct. 20, 1885

Name of Deceased.	Age at Death			Date of Death.
	Years.	Months.	Days.	
Brown, Nathaniel,	28	——	——	June 19, 1828
Harriet,	82	——	——	Feb. 11, 1884
Chas. L.,	24	——		Nov. 15, 1847
Mary A. S.,	34	——		July 4, 1859
Wm. Augustus,	28	10	17	Nov. 16, 1833
Ruth,	22	——		May 1, 1801
Nathaniel,	29			May 31, 1794
Rebekah,	96			July 15, 1805
Buck, Daniel,				Mch. 18, 1837
Frances E.,		5	17	Oct. 10, 1839
James F.,	74			1888
Hancy M.,	——			1843
James R.,	25			July 24, 1865
Alida Maria,	-			1866
Willietta,				1869
Wilbur E.,	46	——		1891
Barnard B.,	70	——	-	Mch. 20, 1875
Desire,	80	——		Dec. 29, 1890
Hatsel N.,	——	-		Mch 3, 1799
Martha E.,	2	8		Sept. 1, 1848
Earl A.,	2	8		Apr. 14, 1860
Olin H.,	6	8		Apr. 24, 1860
Horace B.,	74			Apr. 25, 1896
Erastus,	41			Aug. 23, 1839
Eunice,	59			Mch. 7, 1859
Mary,	89		--	Mch. 18, 1874
Isaac,	22		--	Jan. 26, 1829
James,	63		-	Jan. 8, 1838
Ruth,	80			Aug. 12, 1857
Hannah,	——	——	——	Mch. 1831
Miss M.,	——	——	——	Oct. 16, 1836
Justus,	-	——	——	Feb. 5, 1837
Buckingham, Sam. S.,	62	——	——	Jan. 3, 1870
Julia R.,	49	——	——	Apr. 2, 1863
Rosella E.,	43	——	——	Mch. 28, 1875
Jane,	4	——	——	Sept. 4, 1841
Joseph,	1	3	——	Dec. 3, 1845
Isabel W.,	3	——	——	Feb. 15, 1869
Herman,	16	——	——	Jan. 29, 1866
Emma K.,	33	——	——	Feb. 27, 1868
Jennie,	27	——		Mch. 18, 1869
Bunce, Mary,	——	——		Jan. 30, 1803
Julia C.,	43	-		Dec. 4, 1876
Mrs. T.,	——		——	Mch. 22, 1804

Name of Deceased.	Age at Death.			Date of Death.
	Years.	Months.	Days.	
Burgsson, Nelson,	--	---	---	Feb. 4, 1888
Burton, Lydia,	23	---	---	July 30, 1780
Lucy,	20		—	Nov. 6, 1779
Button, Wilbur F.,	—	---	—	Feb 23, 1852
Willard F.,	—		—	Feb. 23, 1852
Jeremiah,	70	—	---	June 2, 1861
Jeremiah P.,	62	—	---	Sept. 10, 1889
Clarissa,	74	--	---	June 5. 1861
Lorinda,	47	—	—	Mch. 15, 1863
Sally,	—	—	—	Oct. 11, 1813
Fanny,	---	---	—	Aug. 28, 1821
Mary,	---	---	—	Oct. 26, 1813
Daniel,	69	---	--	Aug. 20, 1892
Harriet W.,	—	—	—	Sept. 25, 1889
Egbert O.,	---	—	--	April 3. 1893
Mary S.,	66			Dec. 17, 1888
John,	---			Nov. 24, 1826
Emily,	--	-		Feb. 28, 1831
John,				May 8, 1836
William,				Feb. 28, 1826

Whole No. B's, 186.

C

Name of Deceased.	Years.	Months.	Days.	Date of Death.
Campbell, Olive,	56			Mch. 3, 1826
Case, Harley,	84	3	—	Jan. 20, 1894
Harriet M.,	70	9		Oct. 6, 1889
Diantha,	82	---		1891
William,	76			Dec. 9. 1844
Phebe,	90	.		Feb. 23, 1865
Cashean, Mr.,	—		---	July 23, 1805
Cay, Mr.,	--		—	Oct 10, 1814
Chase, Nellie,	24	---	—	June 14, 1888
Chapman, Mrs. W.,	.	—		Feb. 20, 1827
Ira,		-	---	Dec. 1820
Anna,			---	Jan. 4, 1818
Cheney, Chas.,	3	—	---	Sept. 21, 1776
Prudence,	20	—	---	Aug. 8, 1771
Elizabeth,	4	—	—	May 23. 1775
Asahel,	--	6	—	Mch. 28, 1786
Daniel,	60	—	—	Oct. 1, 1820
Julia,	28	---	---	Mch. 12, 1790
Jemima,	73	—	---	May 9, 1836

Name of Deceased.	Age at Death			Date of Death
	Years.	Months.	Days.	
Cheney, Sarah A.,	64	—	-	Mch 1, 1870
Daniel,	48	—		Apr. 18, 1850
Lucy,	4	—		Sept. 18, 1776
Churchel, Daniel,	60	—		June 27, 1770
Bethiah,	76	—	-	July 20, 1779
John,	70	—		Apr. 13, 1773
Churchill, Joseph,	63	—		Dec 19, 1797
Prudence,	68	—		May 1, 1799
Charles,	40			Aug. 19, 1844
Mary H.,	2	-		Oct. 25, 1824
Maria,	—	7	4	May 3, 1796
Ruth,	82			Jan. 11, 1849
Chas.,	71			Apr. 21, 1840
Joseph,	17			Feb. 16, 1824
Ruth,	20			Dec. 30, 1818
Laura,	19			June 1815
Joseph B.,		13		Aug. 11, 1805
Joseph,	63			Dec. 19, 1797
Chas.,				
Mrs ,				Oct. 17, 1805
Clark, Daniel,				Dec. 25, 1832
Peleg,				Sept. 8, 1832
Peleg R.,	-			Feb. 24, 1836
John H.,	67			June 11, 1892
Sarah J.,	63		-	Mch. 1, 1895
Norman C.,	25	6	-	Mch. 30, 1884
Chas. W.,	1			Feb. 11, 1880
Coles, Joseph,	80	-		Dec. 18, 1867
Percy,	66			Nov. 23, 1862
Charley,	2	6		Oct. 14, 1842
Cole, Mrs. L.,	—	—		Oct. 9, 1803
Colton, Elijah,	85			May 7, 1853
Nabby,	42			Aug. 19, 1831
Edmund,	20			Oct. 1834
Sarah,	48			
Mrs.,	98		-	Nov. 1, 1823
Elizabeth S.,	80		—	Nov. 24, 1897
Concklin, Henry S.,	78	4	—	Aug. 26, 1881
Sarah B.,	61	2	10	Dec. 11, 1871
Lydia A. H.,	72	—	—	July 6, 1895
John A.,	70	-	—	July 30, 1879
Harriet B.,	74	-	-	Aug. 17, 1855
Isaac,	44	-	-	Feb. 26, 1824
Harriet,	42	—	—	Mch. 10, 1889

Name of Deceased.	Age at Death.			Date of Death.
	Years.	Months.	Days.	
Concklin, Catharine,	83	—	—	Mch. 8, 1890
Elizabeth,	46	—	—	Feb. 12, 1866
Richard B.,	74	—	—	Sept. 8, 1887
Conklin, Alfred H.,	20	—	—	Feb. 9, 1853
Cone, Caroline M ,	-	—	—	Nov. 19, 1890
Cook, Harriet F.,	35	—	—	Feb. 24, 1862
Mrs. A.,	—	—	—	Nov. 27, 1817
Mrs.,		—	—	Oct. 19, 1814
Cooper, Sally G.,	45	.	—	Oct. 29, 1849
Lydia M.,	5	-	-	Sept. 19, 1849
Mortimer,	10	—	—	Oct. 3, 1849
Mrs.,	—	—	—	July 31, 1798
Mary,	72	—	—	July 30, 1798
Cornwall, Mary,	-	.	—	Dec. 19, 1816
Erick,	-	—	-	Jan. 26, 1814
Mrs. T.,	-	—	-	Dec. 20, 1815
Sarah,	-	—	—	Nov. 17, 1795
Geo.,	—			Oct. 17, 1824
David,	84	—		May 3, 1874
Anna,	77	—		July 11, 1855
Julia A.,	32			Dec. 7, 1851
Maria A ,	73		—	Oct. 14, 1869
Elizabeth,	60		—	Nov. 18, 1881
Ezra,	64		.	Dec. 22, 1851
Carrie,			—	July 14, 1881
Amos,	70	—	—	Feb. 24, 1871
Sybil,	74	—	—	Oct. 18, 1875
Chas. F.,	51	-	—	June 2, 1885
Esther A.,	53	.	—	Sept. 29, 1887
Harvey B.,	65	—	—	June 11, 1889
Jeannette L. G.,	64	—	—	Apr. 4, 1893
Minnie A.,	6	9	—	Aug. 14, 1866
Jessie B.,	31	6	—	Mch. 7, 1889
James H.,	39	—	—	Aug. 31, 1896
Mary E.,	9	—	—	Feb. 1, 1869
Nellie E.,	15	.	.	Sept. 15, 1894
Andrew,	72	—	—	July 7, 1894
Timothy,	45	—	—	Mch. 12, 1837
Thomas,	81	—	—	Oct. 13, 1831
Mary,	51	—	—	Nov. 16, 1812
Andrew,	40	—	—	Nov. 2, 1799
Andrew,	33	—	—	July 18, 1768
Samuel,	72	—	—	Apr. 18, 1829
Rachel,	78	—	—	Aug. 6, 1841

Name of Deceased.	Age at Death.			Date of Death.		
	Years.	Months.	Days.			
Cornwall, Jemima,	69	—	—	Apr.	3,	1850
Harvey,	78	—	—	Mch.	8,	1868
Maria A.,	66	—	—	Oct.	20,	1884
Cynthia,	42	—	—	Dec.	9,	1897
Cornwell, Susanna,	27	—	—	June	2,	1788
Moley,	1	2	—	Dec.	23,	1772
Mime,	1	2	—	Nov.	7,	1769
Jerusha,	38	—	—	May	30,	1793
Moses,	34	—	—	Oct.	14,	1777
Sally,	4	—	—	Dec.	11,	1772
Cornwall, Asa,	1	9	—	June	6,	1775
Nathaniel,	73	—	—	Mch.	22,	1823
Anna,	90	—	—	Sept.	29,	1848
Baby,	—	—	4	Aug.	10,	1890
Esther,	—	—	—			
Polly,	—	—	—			
Thomas,	—	—	—			
Corwick, Joseph,	—	—	—	Sept.	1,	1883
Cotton, Thaddeus,	—	—	—	July	6,	1800
Hosea,	—	—	—	April	17,	1857
Cox, George,	—	—	—			
Isaac,	65	—	—	Sept.	15,	1890
George,	70	—	—	Oct.	2,	1880
Eliza B.,	69	—	—	Apr.	1,	1890
Geo. W.,	—	3	5	May	20,	1890
Crittenden, Daniel,	69	10	—	Jan.	4,	1887
Jane G.,	63	—	—	Sept.	18,	1888
David,	72	—	—	Oct.	14,	1888
Catharine,	73	—	—	Jan.	11,	1878
Edward G.,	13	—	—	July	2,	1891
Jessie,	—	10	—	Oct.	16,	1886
Jennie,	—	8	—	Aug.	3,	1886
George,	44	—	—	Sept.	20,	1852
Anne E.,	86	—	—	May	10,	1891
Mary L.,	38	—	—	Jan.	1,	1875
Randolph,	7	—	—	Jan.	27,	1841
Francis,	—	—	8	July	18,	1841
Charles,	30	—	—	Dec.	18,	1844
Olive Martha,	85	10	—	Sept.	28,	1881
Julia D.,	8	9	18	Nov.	4,	1859
Atwell B.,	—	6	—	Jan.	14,	1844
Daniel,	—	—	—	Jan.	9,	1815
Daniel,	80	—	—	Feb.	4,	1824
Rhoda,	83	—	—	Dec.	22,	1828

Name of Deceased.	Age at Death.			Date of Death.
	Years.	Months.	Days.	
Crittenden, David,	81	—	—	May 16, 1859
Elizabeth,	40	—	—	Dec. 19, 1821
Jemima,	87	—	—	June 29, 1859
Daniel,	6	—	—	Sept. 2, 1773
Ansel,			—	Mch. 8, 1814
Mrs.,				Dec. 12, 1808
Crosby, Molly,	3	—		1774
Prudence,	78	—		July 4, 1823
Mrs.,				July 15, 1824
John,				Apr. 17, 1810
Crouch, Lois,				Aug. 4, 1878
Mary,				
Joseph,				
Culver, Martin,	69			Dec. 29, 1867
Lucy P. B.,	91			July 17, 1894
Dolly Ann,	2	3		Nov. 8, 1841
Lucy A.,	6			Dec. 4, 1831
Wm. Alonzo.,		7	19	Feb. 17, 1878
Annie,	11	8		Oct. 5, 1880
Emma,	5	8		Feb. 17, 1878

Whole No. C's. 171.

D

Davis, Chas.,	44			Aug. 22, 1819
Seth J.,	69	9	—	Aug. 11, 1877
Zerviah,	70	5		Aug. 25, 1880
Sarah M.,	66			Apr. 18, 1896
Mary E. B.,	35		—	Sept. 27, 1850
Sally,			—	Aug. 30, 1819
Martha,			—	Sept. 7, 1819
Ann,				Apr. 6, 1882
Mary E.,		14		July 20, 1851
Day, Mary A. L.,	28	—	—	Sept. 11, 1851
Isaac H.,	84		—	Apr. 29, 1862
Sarah E. W.,	74			Apr. 1, 1890
Sparrow W.,	31	—	—	Dec. 4, 1877
Daniels, Frances E.,	—	—		
Demay, Heman,	29	—	—	May 31, 1863
Eudora,	42	—	—	June 13, 1879
Deming, Eliza,	—	—		June 6, 1870
Denison, Eliza A.,	56	—		Oct. 29, 1855
Dewa, Mrs.,	—	—		Dec. 2, 1818
Mrs.,	—	—	—	July 13, 1811

Name of Deceased.	Age at Death.			Date of Death.
	Years.	Months.	Days.	
Dixon, John,	—	—		May 8, 1836
Nabby,	—	—	—	Feb. 15, 1807
Dikson, Chas.,	5	—		Aug. 24, 1783
Dixson, Edward,	—	9		Jan. 16, 1779
Dixon, Wm ,	81	-		Mch. 20, 1826
Prudence,	70	- -		Sept. 20, 1821
Robert,	5			Aug. 15, 1821
Wm. L.,	70			Mch. 4, 1877
Hannah,	- -	—	—	
Caroline,	—	- -	—	Dec. 28, 1825
Daniel,	—	—	—	Aug. 31, 1796
Amanda,	—			Feb. 6, 1809
Dickinson, Ira,	81	10	21	Mch. 18, 1877
Dolittle, Margaret,	—	—		June 6, 1870
Margaret,		- -		Apr. 1, 1814
Dudley, Abby,	35	9	18	Sept. 14, 1843
Dunham, Daniel E.,	78	—	—	Sept. 11, 1892
E. D.,	28		—	Nov. 3, 1864
Mary S.,	53		-	Nov. 23, 1861
John E.,	45			Nov. 19, 1864
Edwin G.,	36			Apr. 7, 1860
Julia A.,	25			Sept. 15, 1850
Jacob,	80			Sept. 21, 1867
Harriet G.,	79	-		Aug. 8, 1870
Orrilla.	80	8		Dec. 23, 1897

Whole No. D's, 45.

E

Evans, Wm. H.,	53	-		Dec. 14, 1880
Adaline M.,	51	- -		Mch. 21, 1885
Adaline A.,	87			May 30, 1897
Harvey,	-			Nov. 29, 1894
Ellen E.,	- -	-		Apr. 27, 1881
Henry,				July 7, 1877
Eddy, Thomas,	30			Sept. 26, 1829
Esther,	75			Feb. 19, 1829
Thomas,	64		—	Jan. 24, 1814
Bethiah,	66			July 17, 1789
Caroline,	64			July 31, 1851
William,	—			Sept. 15, 1870
Lydia,	70			Sept. 20, 1851
Seth,	99		-	Sept. 28, 1845
Edwards, Solomon B.,	66	—		July 27, 1878

Name of Deceased.	Age at Death.			Date of Death.
	Years.	Months.	Days.	
Edwards, Rachel M.,	61	—	—	Apr. 5, 1869
George,	21	—	—	Sept. 4, 1864
Ellsworth, Sarah,	30	—	—	Mch. 14, 1770
Samuel C.,	—	6	—	Nov. 11, 1768
Samuel C.,	—	4	—	May 22, 1770
Maria,	—	—	17	May 7, 1789
Emmons, Lawrence,	—	—	—	Feb. 6, 1870

Whole No. E's, 22.

F

Name of Deceased.	Years.	Months.	Days.	Date of Death.
Fessenden, Edward,	—	6	—	Sept. 15, 1821
Henry H.,				Jan. 12, 1896
Elizabeth,				May 12, 1894
Thomas,	—			
Harriet,				Nov. 22, 1881
Augusta,				Nov. 26, 1881
Mrs. Thos.,				Nov. 25, 1832
Fenn, Lucy B.,	37	—		Oct. 9, 1858
Fisk, Benjamin,	—	—		Mch. 1, 1802
Field, Prudence,	77	—		Mch. 27, 1877
Flavell, Marion E.,	29			Aug. 30, 1892
Flint, James,	—			Jan. 9, 1880
Mary,		—		Nov. 11, 1886
Sissy,				
Mary,		—	14	Mch. 20, 1843
Martha,		—	28	Apr. 5, 1843
Foster, Whitby,	43	—	—	Oct. 14, 1853
Sarah S.,	34	—		Oct. 8, 1853
Isaac,	50			May 2, 1833
Prudence,	73			Dec. 25, 1858
Nelson P.,	39			Mch. 16, 1853
Fox, Silence,	93			Feb. 16, 1784
Caroline D.,	—	—		June 23, 1888
Fowler, Jane R.,	55	—		June 7, 1890
Fuller, Mrs.,	29	—		Feb 16, 1859

Whole No. F's, 25.

G

Name of Deceased.	Years.	Months.	Days.	Date of Death.
Giddings, James,	59	—		Nov. 5, 1851
Martha,	59	—		Oct. 24, 1850
Harriet,	32	—		July 12, 1823
John,				Sept. 20, 1809
Mrs. J.,				Sept. 11, 1808

Name of Deceased.	Age at Death.			Date of Death.
	Years.	Months.	Days.	
Gilbert, Dr. G. C. H.,	72			Oct. 30, 1889
Harriet Talcott,	71			Jan. 30, 1897
C. H.,	37			May 21, 1883
Gildersleeve,				
Temperance,	75	5	13	Sept. 22, 1831
Philip,	65	3	24	Oct. 26, 1822
*Mary,	73			June 24, 1798
Obadiah,	88			Jan. 5, 1816
Richard,	17			Mch. 21, 1782
Nancy,	88			Aug. 7, 1893
Jeremiah,	75	7		Mch. 16, 1857
Lucy,	81			Dec. 22, 1860
Temperance,	27			Oct. 13, 1836
Sylvester,	91		18	Mch. 15, 1886
Rebecca,	30	2		Aug. 10, 1824
Emily (Shepard),	72	11	24	July 14, 1877
Lavalette,			10	Dec. 16, 1841
Philip,	42			June 12, 1884
Sylvester S.,	23	1	1	Oct. 2, 1852
Adelaide E.,	35	0	16	Sept. 28, 1880
Philip,		5		Oct. 21, 1850
Henry,	77		2	Apr. 9, 1894
Emily F.,	54			Nov. 11, 1873
Nancy,	30			Mch. 14, 1842
Emily S.,	2			Mch. 2, 1842
Annah S.,	4			Aug. 27, 1854
Mary S.,	3			Oct. 18, 1851
Susan,		5		June 8, 1853
Philip,	34	3	7	Oct. 12, 1853
Anna D.,	30			Jan. 19, 1854
Emily H.,		14		Aug. 12, 1880
Elizabeth J.,		7		Jan. 18, 1883
Gillum, Isabella G.,	21	10		May 23, 1855
Gladwin, Joseph C.,	67			Sept. 1, 1896
Erasmus,	88			July 12, 1889
Prudence,	74			Nov. 12, 1883
Julia R.,	42			Dec. 13, 1879
Helen,	7			Jan. 12, 1871
F. Leroy,		4		Aug. 30, 1874
Gleason, Mrs.,				May 14, 1880
Goodel, Henry,				Jan. 31, 1805
Goodrich, Nathan,				Apr. 21, 1857
Ralph,	56			June 24, 1846
Rachel,	64			Sept. 21, 1863

*Inscription in the family Bible gives date of death, June 2, 1797.

Name of Deceased	Age at Death.			Date of Death.
	Years.	Months.	Days.	
Goodrich, Chas.,	24		—	Oct. 11, 1841
Jabez,			-	Sept. 10, 1789
Joseph,			—	1787
Susannah,	94		—	Aug. 31, 1821
Chas..	86		. .	July 15, 1807
Phebe,	76	—		Dec. 11, 1850
Amos,	81	. .		June 15, 1845
Katharine,	32			July 7, 1797
Lucy,	63	—		Mch. 21, 1813
Anna,	56	- -		July 30, 1805
Hezekiah,	72	—	.	Apr. 21, 1817
Submit,	40	- -	.	Dec. 22, 1787
Sophronia,	30	- -	-	Jan. 25, 1815
Jeremiah,	81	.	—	July 14, 1823
Hepzibah,	31	- -	- -	Nov. 23, 1796
David,	15	- -	- -	Jan. 31, 1794
Jeremiah,	84		-	May 8, 1793
Ruth,	69	-	—	Sept. 11, 1778
Rebecca,	76		-	June 10, 1833
Joseph,	69		.	Feb. 7, 1852
Susan,	70		. .	July 10, 1853
Eunice S.,	7			Feb. 17, 1828
Hepzibah,	3	7		Mch. 1, 1816
Oliver,	—	7		Feb. 17, 1811
Reuben,	36			Jan. 20, 1798
Gershom,	73			June 18, 1789
Richard,	48			Mch. 11, 1767
Jeremiah J.,	2	10		May 21, 1821
Russell,	4			Dec. 27, 1801
Hannah,	72			Nov. 24, 1801
Joshua,	70			Oct. 23, 1792
Joseph E.,	72			Oct. 8, 1879
Nancy W..	80			Dec. 30, 1891
Sarah W..	18			Oct. 16, 1866
Nancy M.,	20	10		Jan. 29, 1871
William,	65			Nov. 18, 1870
Lucy A. G..	71			Sept. 7, 1878
Lucy A. G..	17			Sept. 29, 1858
Hellen V..	5			Nov. 31, 1839
Patrick H.,	- -	3		May 15, 1839
John Q..	45			June 17, 1890
Hepzibah E..,	45			Dec. 27, 1894
Joseph,	66		-	Mch. 27, 1880
H. Sherman,	37			Jan. 23, 1875
Sophia A..,	2			Oct. 5, 1849

Name of Deceased.	Age at Death			Date of Death.
	Years.	Months.	Days.	
Goodrich, Mary A..	37			Feb. 11, 1807
Elsie M.,	1	2		Dec. 12, 1891
Fannie A..	77			July 20, 1897
Geo. G.,	76			Aug. 25, 1895
Chester,	83			Sept. 22, 1881
Rebecca B.,	78	11		Mch. 21, 1876
Martha,				Dec. 13, 1797
Mary S.,	57			May 2, 1892
Elizabeth,				May 25, 1805
Lydia,				Aug. 26, 1810
Solomon,				Apr. 8, 1804
Belinda,				
Goff, Norman A.,		2	11	Mch. 31, 1857
Emeline S.,	27	---		Apr. 6, 1855
Francis E..	---	2	6	Feb. 27, 1864
Jerusha,		---		May 4, 1799
Nellie,				Sept. 21, 1886
Gideon,			--	Apr. 4, 1795
Graham, Joseph,	--			Sept. 30, 1807

Whole No. G's, 112.

H

Hale, Eunice,				Apr. 24, 1835
Azariah,	15		---	July 12, 1839
Alexander,	57			Oct. 2, 1849
Daniel,	66			May 2, 1828
Lydia,	78			June 29, 1839
Dorothy,			---	
Geo. Jr.,	30			Nov. 18, 1841
Daniel,	79			Apr. 18, 1897
Hattie F.,				Apr. 26, 1895
Mary G.,		10	23	Jan. 4, 1802
Georgeanna B.	4	10	16	Dec. 3, 1893
Nabby,				May 15, 1877
Emily,	2			Feb. 19, 1871
Isabel,	---	8	---	Sept. 3, 1874
Edwin,	---			June 19, 1885
Johnnie,	13	9		July 10, 1885
Oliver M.,	43			Oct. 17, 1889
Sophronia M.,	61			Apr. 4, 1880
Warren E.,	---	8		Oct. 29, 1803
James A. Jr.,	20	---		Sept. 13, 1884
David,	61			Oct. 27, 1802

Name of Deceased.	Age at Death.			Date of Death
	Years.	Months.	Days.	
Hale, Henry,	31	—	—	Sept. 7, 1870
Sarah,	80	—	—	May 26, 1884
David,	67	—	—	Jan. 26, 1892
Chas. D.,	—	5	—	Oct. 11, 1860
Francis,	65	—	—	Apr. 9, 1888
Katie F. S.,	34	—	—	Dec. 10, 1894
David,	—	—		May 11, 1805
Mrs. F.,				Mch. 17, 1887
Elisha,		—	July 15, 1836
Frederick,	—	—	Oct. 10, 1894
John H.,	9			Sept. 20, 1860
Anna S.,	95	7	—	May 1, 1885
Geo.,				Mch. 26, 1869
Ruth,				Nov. 7, 1877
Elisha,			July 13, 1805
Mrs. E.,		—	May 21, 1822
Mrs.,		—	Mch 23, 1815
Mrs. E.,			June 25, 1817
Haling, Jennie,	22	—		Aug. 6, 1883
Dora F.,	1	3		Nov. 7, 1883
Joseph,			—	Mch. 27, 1837
Hall, Nelson,		—	July 3, 1874
Mrs. N.,		—	Nov. 12, 1887
Ruth,	57		—	1877
Ebenezer,	67		—	1863
Laura C.,	75			1871
Elizabeth	1		—	1843
William,	1	3		July 31, 1835
Adelaide,	—	10		Aug. 20, 1851
Abner,	84	—		Apr. 17, 1885
Eliza,	73	—		June 23, 1874
Abner Jr.,	43	—		Sept. 4, 1868
Jane E.,	46	—		July 4, 1882
Hattie C.,	24			Feb. 26, 1863
Jabez,	56			1837
Mrs. J.,			—	Aug. 3, 1826
David,	6	6		Mch. 22, 1818
David,	19			Feb. 25, 1838
Almira,	16			Oct. 30, 1830
Samuel,	3			Apr. 8, 1774
David,	53			July 17, 1894
Amos,	4			Feb. 23, 1774
Amos,	11			July 27, 1785
Lucy,	71		—	Apr. 3, 1814

Name of Deceased.	Years.	Months.	Days.	Date of Death.
Hall, Isaac,	78		—	Apr. 3, 1819
Mrs. Isaac,	70	—	-	Sept. 5, 1778
Sarah,	—	-		Sept. 7, 1803
Wm. B.,	—			Oct. 18, 1825
Mary,	93			1882
Mrs. T.,	—		-	Dec. 7, 1815
Harvey, Rev. W. N.,	64		—	Jan. 8, 1889
Hastings, Betsey C.,	37		—	Feb. 20, 1804
Heart, Charlotte,	80	-	-	July 8, 1865
Holbrook, Eleanor,	-			May 25, 1897
Hopkins, Godfrey,	63	-		Apr. 26, 1834
Pillina,	59	-		June 24, 1830
Elmer R.,	3	—		Aug. 5, 1864
Hancy M.,	16	1		Oct. 15, 1861
Leonard B.,	12	6		Nov. 17, 1861
Mima B.,	44	—		May 3, 1850
Ebenezer M.,	73	10	10	June 6, 1887
Russell,	80	-		Feb. 28, 1878
Hannah,	42			Apr. 29, 1841
Fanny S.,	77		—	Dec. 21, 1895
Russell L.,	22	-	—	Oct. 21, 1850
Martha D.,	40	—	—	July 22, 1888
Henry,	—	—	35	Aug. 5, 1888
Russell F.,	—	6	10	July 10, 1874
Daniel F.,	63	10	23	Apr. 14, 1871
Maranda,	32	—	—	1835
Hubbard, Anna,	91	—	—	Jan. 21, 1779
Catharine,	52	—	—	Feb. 26, 1868
Sarah A.,	—	—	—	Jan 16, 1895
Edmund,	—	—	—	Feb. 9, 1883
Emily,	36	—	—	Feb. 29, 1864
Thomas,	—	—	—	Sept. 24, 1873
Huber, John,	—	—	—	July 30, 1869
Hurlbut, Mary E.,	21	—	—	July 24, 1860
Chester,	87	—	—	May 1, 1896
Julia,	—	—	—	Mch. 18, 1886
Henry B.,	—	8	—	Aug. 16, 1883
Howard R.,	3	5	—	Feb. 27, 1884
Seymour,	83	-	—	Oct. 1, 1873
Asenath,	77	-	—	Feb. 13, 1870
Simeon,	56	—	—	Apr. 12, 1877
Alanson A.,	63	—	—	Mch. 28, 1863
Charlotte S.,	48	—	—	Jan. 8, 1862
Ruba M.,	21	—	—	Sept. 10, 1860

Name of Deceased.	Age at Death.			Date of Death.
	Years.	Months.	Days.	
Hurlbut, Agnes D.,	23	—		Nov. 14, 1864
David,	66	—	—	Sept. 6, 1868
Electa A.,	66	—		Sept. 30, 1878
Harriet S.,	13	—		Nov. 14, 1825
Clarence S.,	2	3		Jan. 5, 1859
Helen M.,	5	9		July 27, 1865
Anna M.,	1	5	22	Dec. 27, 1876
Sarah J.,	29	—	—	Apr. 10, 1891
Seymour,	28	—	—	Apr. 17, 1896
Seymour,	84	—	—	Nov. 29, 1840
Deborah,	85	—	—	Apr. 28, 1840
Jesse,	98	—	—	Jan. 7, 1870
Lucy,	68		—	May 3, 1843
Chester S.,	—	—	35	Apr. 1, 1841
Gideon,	94	—	—	July 1, 1823
Deborah,	87	—	—	Dec. 14, 1819
Eliza,		—	—	
Hills, Sarah,		—	—	Mch. 3, 1879
Chauncy,		—	—	

Whole No. H's, 128

I

Ilsley, John A.,	74	—	—	Dec. 4, 1896
Arvilla D.,	80	—	—	Apr. 16, 1897
Ingraham, John,	54	—		Jan. 25, 1848

Whole No. I's, 3.

J

Johnson, Jesse,	5		—	Oct. 11, 1775
Jesse,	4		—	Apr. 16, 1780
Jonas,	—		—	Nov. 17, 1883
Jones, Sarah M.,	43		—	Oct. 11, 1886
Hattie M,	12	8	—	June 24, 1877

Whole No. J's, 5.

K

Name of Deceased.	Age at Death.			Date of Death.
	Years.	Months.	Days.	
Kelsey, Oliver D.,	45	—		Aug. 15, 1872
Catherine B.,	27	-		Sept. 4, 1861
Charles,	3	-		Aug. 21, 1864
Frances M.,	62	—		Dec. 20, 1896
Elizabeth L.,	10	—		Oct. 15, 1869
Julia P.,	15	8		July 26, 1888
Frederick M.,	1	5	15	Feb. 15, 1868
Isabel A.,	1	6	—	Aug. 24, 1854
Charlie J.,	—	9		Oct. 4, 1858
Kelleg, Wm.,	—	-		Sept. 18, 1829
Kilborn, Caroline,	-	—	-	Jan. 30, 1821
Kilby, Jane A.,	28	—	—	Feb. 28, 1854
Knowles, Silence,	75	—	—	Mch. 20, 1840
Amos,	14	—		Feb. 21, 1802
John,	58	—	—	Mch. 25, 1840
Abraham,	35			Sept. 28, 1771
Kyes, Mercy,	—			Nov. 9, 1812

Whole No. K's, 17.

L

Lawrence, William,				
Isabella,		11	10	Sept. 4, 1858
Agnes M.,	6	6	15	April 4, 1862
Marion H.,	4	—	10	Aug. 7, 1863
Willie,	—	—	3	May 7, 1864
William,	26	—	—	May, 1895
Lawson, Christina C.,	32	—	—	June 29, 1882
Lewis, Abel,	73	—	-	Oct. 15, 1845
Mary,	53	—	—	Jan. 31, 1829
Bartlett,	46	—	-	Sept. 10, 1853
Anna,	38	—	-	May 8, 1828
George,	78	-	—	Mch. 29, 1826
Elizabeth,	63		—	Jan. 29, 1815
George,	77		-	Jan. 13, 1796
Bathsheba,	84			Jan. 29, 1805
George,	—	6		Oct. 11, 1794
Ida Jane,	4	—		Dec. 10, 1863
Wm. G.,	72	-		Sept. 25, 1875

Name of Deceased.	Years.	Age at Death, Months.	Days.	Date of Death
Lewis, Mary R.,	70	—	—	Jan. 23, 1876
Edward,	76	—	—	Nov. 5, 1870
Cynthia,	62	10	19	Feb. 16, 1860
Amelia,	82	-	—	Nov. 15, 1893
Mary,	85	—	—	Feb. 21, 1868
William,	62	—		Feb. 9, 1872
Mary S.,	61	—		Oct. 20, 1876
Mary S.,	25		—	Oct. 31, 1879
Lincoln, Sarah,	57	—	-	Oct. 6, 1887
Julia A. C.,		—		Apr. 29, 1893
Loveland, Orlanza,	62	—		Dec. 28, 1879
Sarah S.,	72	—	-	June 22, 1890
Eddie O.,	5	—		July 24, 1862
Lord, Wm. C.,	1	—		Oct. 6, 1805
Lucas, Carrie,	-			Nov. 4, 1881
Lorton, John,	—			Dec. 8, 1857

Whole No. L's, 34.

M

	Years.	Months.	Days.	Date of Death
Maddon, Paul,		—	—	Aug. 9, 1885
Martin, Alexander,		—	—	May 25, 1876
Matthews, Hiram,		—	-	Dec. 25, 1881
Phebe,	—	-	—	Jan. 5, 1877
Matson, Lucy,	46	—	—	July 17, 1828
Mackauney, Wm.,	—	—	—	July 15, 1797
McCormick, Geo.,	-	—	—	Feb. 13, 1895
Annie Ellen,	14	—		Sept. 29, 1896
Mighles, John,	34	—		Feb. 7, 1777
Miller, David,	—	—	49	Nov. 5, 1795
Amelia D.,	41	—	—	Aug. 29, 1838
John C.,	—	8	18	Aug. 24, 1845
George,	6	—	—	
George,	—	-	42	
Mitchell, Mary L.,	—	—	—	Dec. 15, 1895
McKay, John,	42	—	—	Feb. 2, 1894
Angus,	29	—	—	Apr. 30, 1854
Montgomery, Mrs. N.,	—	—	—	Feb. 17, 1801
Morgan, Phebe,	—	—	—	Nov. 22, 1883
Samuel,	—	—	—	Oct. 8, 1887
Mosher, George,	61	—	-	Mch. 28, 1896

Name of Deceased	Age at Death.			Date of Death
	Years.	Months.	Days.	
Mosher, Phebe J.,	62			Jan. 23, 1897
Myrick, Alfred,	66			Aug. 25, 1862
Esther,	48			Mch. 15, 1824

Whole No. M's, 24.

N

Naongren, Lars,	–	–	–	Oct. 27, 1883
Neff, Mary W.,	38	—	–	Sept. 12, 1887
Neland, Mr.,	– –	–	– –	Aug. 10, 1796
Rebecca,			—	May 15, 1811
Nelson, Mrs.,	—	–	– –	Jan. 1, 1889
Nicholls, Nannie,	4	4	26	Apr. 18, 1889
Nicholson, Chas. C.,	4	7	– –	Mch. 22, 1879
Norcott, Wm.,	56	– –		Mch. 6, 1823
Dorcas,	83	– –		Apr. 20, 1856
Emily,	64	—		Mch. 27, 1870
Elijah,	54	–		July 14, 1854
Frederick,	7			June 20, 1845
Mary J.,	25	—	– –	Sept. 25, 1859
Wm.,	83	5	–	Aug. 4, 1886
Mary,	69	11	—	Nov. 27, 1882
Emma E.,	– –	5	—	July 14, 1872
Lillie,	1	4	– –	Dec. 26, 1874
Chas. A.,	26	6	—	Aug. 12, 1874
Richard,	54	—	—	Mch. 8, 1869
Henry P.,	2	1	—	Sept. 21, 1849
Harvey,	—	—	—	
Northam, Ralph,	47	—	—	Jan. 8, 1871
Oliver,	75	– –	—	Apr. 2, 1869
Sophia S.,	83	—	—	Nov. 26, 1877

Whole No. N's, 24.

O

Osborne, Cynthia,	64	– –	—	Mch. 8, 1837
Overton, Gen. Seth.,	94	– –	– –	Aug. 17, 1852
Mehetable W.,	74	– –	– –	Aug. 20, 1828
Augustin,	65	– –	—	Dec. 29, 1857
Almira,	83	– –	—	Aug. 8, 1874

Name of Deceased.	Age at Death.			Date of Death.
	Years.	Months.	Days.	
Overton, James,	—	—	3	Feb. 27, 1822
Amos C.,	—	8	—	Jan. 11, 1829
Evelyn H.,	66			Oct. 17, 1878
Elton A.,	60		—	Feb. 3, 1880
Emily W.,	76	—	—	
Levantia W.,	58	—	—	
Prudence,	84	—		
Owen, Rachel Drury,	84	—	—	Oct. 17, 1889

Whole No. O's, 13.

P

	Years.	Months.	Days.	
Palmer, Rev. Elliot,	89	—	—	Apr. 4, 1889
Florilla S.,	63	—	—	May 5, 1871
Francis K.,	20	—		
William E.,	21	—		
Chas. H.,	—	2	—	
Thomas A.,	—	2		
Sumner,	-	—	1	
Florilla,	—	—	12	
Loomis T.,	—	18	—	Aug. 23, 1883
Clarence E.,	-	2	—	Aug. 4, 1877
Bertha F.,	2	1	—	Jan. 27, 1877
Nellie E.,	4	2	—	Jan 21, 1877
Loomis,	52	—	—	May 24, 1896
Patten, Nelson,	54	—	—	Oct. 15, 1861
Nelson L.,	19	8	—	July 21, 1856
Eugene L.,	—	11	29	Oct. 29, 1869
Joseph A.,	1	11	29	Dec. 20, 1874
Patterson Luther,	—	—	—	Dec. 22, 1834
Payne, Mimy,	—	—	—	May 22, 1857
Alfred,	73	9	27	Aug. 8, 1861
Amy,	66	11	17	May 20, 1857
Hannah E.,	53	8	20	Mch. 18, 1864
Abbey A.,	28	—	—	Feb. 7, 1867
Mary E. N.,	37	6	—	Nov. 6, 1863
Charlie,	—	2	2	Mch. 8, 1858
Mai Louesa,	8	6	—	July 26, 1881
Anna O.,	32	—	—	Mch. 13, 1893
Job H.,	66	—	—	Aug. 4, 1856
Orilla,	87	—	—	Sept. 13, 1881
Hattie,	43	—	—	Sept. 24, 1880

Name of Deceased	Years	Months	Days	Date of Death
Payne, Lucy W.,	67			Sept. 4, 1885
Almira A.,	63			Aug. 22, 1881
Marion E.,	30			Nov. 16, 1877
Dwight,	—	22		Oct. 5, 1842
Leora,		3		Aug. 3, 1845
Reuben,	70	—		Feb. 27, 1897
Elizabeth,	90	—		July 6, 1853
Anna W.,	35			May 2, 1840
Laura P.,	—	11		June 27, 1886
Leora P.,	—	11		July 1, 1886
Reuben,	48	—		July 31, 1810
Pease, Edward,	59	—		Mch. 14, 1887
Elizabeth,	81			Feb. 23, 1847
Eliza,	19	—		June 24, 1842
Betsey,	73			Nov. 31, 1856
Agift,	79			Oct. 19, 1848
Elizabeth,		3	11	July 25, 1851
Pellet, Nelson B.,	81	—	—	Jan. 17, 1896
Harriet E.,	81			Jan. 27, 1896
Katie E.,	1	9		Nov. 19, 1872
Esther P.,	11	5		June 25, 1873
Chas. N.,	41	—		Nov. 29, 1897
Pelton, Betsey,	84			Aug. 26, 1894
Edward W.,	24			Apr. 1879
Sanford,	75			Jan. 11, 1870
Phebe,	87			Mch. 16, 1883
Arthur H.,	1	3	5	July 1, 1873
Edward F.,	23	—	—	July 20, 1864
Dea. Ralph,	82	8		Feb. 5, 1892
Lydia L.,	53	—		May 4, 1864
Frances A.,	68	6		Nov. 4, 1891
Nelson,	66	—		Nov. 7, 1894
Ettie M.,	24	—		Apr. 8, 1863
Robert W.,	—	3	4	Nov. 4, 1872
Chas. H.,	26	—		June 5, 1864
Lewis,	85			Nov. 8, 1895
Sarah,	68			May 5, 1886
Hannah E.,	47			Feb. 3, 1868
Sophronia,	82			Nov. 15, 1870
Abner,	61			Dec. 20, 1841
Esther,	60			July 13, 1833
Asahel,	17			Aug. 15, 1847
Chester,	43			July 11, 1845
Francis,	—			Aug. 24, 1833

Name of Deceased.	Age at Death.			Date of Death.
	Years.	Months	Days.	
Pelton, Lydia,	42	—	—	Aug. 16, 1847
Anna,	69	—	—	May 19, 1797
Joseph,	83	—	—	Dec. 31, 1804
Asahel,	7	—	—	Apr. 27, 1818
Nabby,	70	—	—	Mch. 12, 1839
Asahel,	75	—	—	July 26, 1843
Mary,	39	—	—	Sept. 8, 1797
Dorothy,	91	—	—	Mch. 2, 1844
Abner,	91	—	—	Jan. 17, 1846
Sarah,	43	—	—	Dec. 8, 1795
Amos,	18	—	—	Oct. 10, 1796
Jeremiah,	37	—	—	July 17, 1822
Philinda,	87	—	—	Apr. 8, 1878
Cynthia,	83	—		Sept. 28, 1880
Marshall,	84	—	—	June 4, 1852
Betsey,	84	—	—	Sept. 1, 1855
Amy C.,	28	—	—	July 28, 1836
Hannah,	82	—	—	June 12, 1810
Josiah,	78	—	—	Feb. 2, 1792
Johnson,	90	—	—	Dec. 13, 1804
Johnson,	84	—	—	Feb. 7, 1839
Rachel,	86	—	—	Mch. 9, 1843
Lucy,	76	—	—	June 2, 1857
Jane R.,	46	—	—	June 4, 1884
Hezekiah G.,	80	—	—	Oct. 20, 1886
Abby T.,	4	—	—	Aug. 19, 1838
Edward B.,	—	15	—	Sept. 2, 1832
Elizabeth A.,	80	—	—	Oct. 20, 1896
Ida E.,	—	—	—	July 14, 1894
Keziah,	—	—	—	Mch. 17, 1814
Julia,	—	—	—	Sept. 4, 1814
Mrs. O.,	—	—	—	Feb. 12, 1828
John,	—	—	—	Nov. 10, 1826
John,	—	—	—	Apr. 17, 1819
Fanny,	—	—	—	June 19, 1819
Mrs. J.,	—	—	—	Feb. 26, 1821
Benjamin,	—	—	—	Aug. 26, 1821
Sally,	—	—	—	Mch. 2, 1825
Mrs. J.,	—	—	—	Mch. 31, 1812
William,	—	—	—	Oct. 9, 1813
Prudence,	—	—	—	July 30, 1833
Pemberton, Patrick G.,	59	—	—	Jan. 28, 1811
Penfield, Mrs.,	—	—	—	Nov. 7, 1803
Mrs. S.,	—	—	—	Mch. 3, 1819

Name of Deceased.	Age at Death			Date of Death.
	Years.	Months.	Days.	
Penfield, Sally,	—	—		Mch. 2, 1835
Prudence,	85	- -		Jan. 12, 1854
Austin A.,	68	6	-	Feb. 11, 1887
Hannah A.,	69	5		Mch. 3, 1892
Emeline E.,	1	10		Sept. 6, 1854
Russell,	75	—		Apr 17. 1869
Abby,	72	-		Sept. 22. 1865
S. Morton,	46	7		Nov. 11, 1872
Samuel,	72	-	---	Oct. 18, 1834
Jemima,	84		—	Dec. 6, 1844
Thaddeus,	42			Sept. 26, 1878
Daniel,	81	—	—	Feb. 7, 1881
Deborah,	57			May 1, 1831
Ruth,	6			Sept. 21, 1799
Jonathan,	68			Mch. 10, 1839
Jane,	57			July 23, 1827
John,	62			Dec. 1, 1829
Simeon,	80			Aug. 25, 1794
Stephen,	36			Sept. 12, 1749
Mary,	90			Jan. 30, 1741
Elizabeth,	--			Dec. 13, 1740
Jonathan,	76			July 23, 1794
Hannah,	17			Apr. 2, 1784
Jonathan,	11			July 19, 1770
Lucia,	8			June 20. 1770
Jonathan,	5			Oct. 1, 1776
Simeon,	91	—		Oct. 7, 1844
Penelope,	59			Mch 22, 1811
Ansel,	26		- -	Feb 24, 1809
Nelson,	4	6		Mch. 14, 1810
Fanny,	- -	4		Oct. 7, 1787
Sarah,	35	-		Sept. 11, 1794
Jonathan,	1	2	—	June 6, 1795
Oliver,	28	-		Apr. 10, 1826
Sarah,	18			Aug. 14, 1834
Zebulon	95	-	---	Jan. 6, 1860
Jonathan,	32			Mch. 30, 1833
Oliver,	7		-	Apr. 11, 1833
John,	67			May 3, 1750
Ruth,	58			July 17, 1794
John,	66			Feb. 22, 1797
Belinda,	—			Feb. 24, 1890
Sophie Y.,	73			Sept. 2, 1887
Alfred C.,	47			Nov. 17, 1856
Francis Joseph,	3			Mch. 6, 1862

| Name of Deceased. | Age at Death. | | | Date of Death. |
	Years.	Months.	Days.	
Penfield, Henry L.,	43	—	—	Jan. 2, 1879
William E.,	2	—	—	Aug. 3, 1840
Emeline B.,	1	—	—	July 28, 1841
Abel,	94	—	—	Mch. 27, 1852
Elizabeth,	77	—	—	May 28, 1837
Horace,	69	—	—	Apr. 8, 1854
Clarissa,	68	—	—	Jan. 22, 1857
Harriet,	73	—	—	Apr. 3, 1888
Chas. H.,	—	8	—	June 10, 1836
Adaline E.,	24	—	—	Dec. 11, 1859
Edgar A.,	—	8	—	Aug. 9, 1860
Almira G.,	49	—	—	Dec. 1, 1889
Hiram A.,	70	—	—	Dec. 19, 1872
Sarah P.,	83	—	—	Feb. 28, 1882
Henry A.,	—	—	49	Feb. 29, 1836
Amos,	—	—	—	Jan. 6, 1826
Esther,	—	—	—	May 30, 1826
John,	—	—	—	Aug. 25, 1808
David,	—	—	—	Feb. 2, 1795
Perkins, Julia A.,	51	—	—	Jan. 15, 1875
Perry, Alice B.,	22	—	—	Sept. 2, 1874
Maxwell,	—	—	33	Aug. 25, 1874
Pitkin, Leonard,	70	—	—	Jan. 31, 1880
Wm. S.,	31	—	—	May 4, 1892
Anna M.,	5	—	—	Aug. 10, 1893
Polly, Thankful,	—	—	—	May 26, 1830
Isaac,	44	—	—	Mch. 12, 1830
Abigail,	84	—	—	Aug. 17, 1864
Sally,	—	—	—	Oct. 1835
Porter, Ezra,	—	—	—	Sept. 9, 1875
Maria,	28	—	—	Apr. 17, 1848
Sarah M.,	—	17	—	Sept. 17, 1850
Sabin,	—	—	—	Mch. 18, 1878
Mary A.,	—	—	—	Apr. 20, 1895
Post, Lucy P. H.,	63	—	—	Apr. 30, 1892
Louisa,	—	—	—	
Pratt, Nellie S.,	13	2	11	Feb. 19, 1889
Willie H.,	—	7	11	May 5, 1868
Preston, Sarah,	—	—	—	Aug. 27, 1860

Whole No. P's, 202.

R

Name of Deceased.	Years.	Months.	Days.	Date of Death.
Rand, Wm.,	—	—	—	Dec. 25, 1878
Chas. W.,	32	—	—	Feb. 5, 1870
I. C.,	—	—	—	
Mary,	—	—	—	May 17, 1875
Randall, Mary V.,	75	—	—	July 15, 1882
Rankin, Freddie,	—	19		Mch. 12, 1854
Ranney, Stephen,	76	—	—	June 7, 1840
Percy,	—	—		June 25, 1854
Julia,	37	—		Jan. 20, 1828
John,	21	—		Feb. 22, 1814
Stephen,	14	—	—	Sept. 5, 1814
Priscilla,	73	—	—	Nov. 27, 1829
David,	57	—	—	Apr. 1, 1813
Huldah L.,	25	—	—	Sept. 5, 1810
John,	—	—	21	Mch. 28, 1830
Jane,	4	9	—	May 30, 1833
William C.,	76	—	—	Apr. 14, 1879
Vienna,	83	10	—	Apr. 27, 1891
Willie,	25	5	—	Dec. 2, 1871
Chas.,	—	—	—	Aug. 15, 1825
Stephen,	—	—	—	June 29, 1800
Mary,	—	—	—	July 22, 1815
Elizabeth,	—	—	—	Sept. 14, 1836
Rathbone, Renselaer,	66	—	—	Dec. 12, 1862
Betsey,	85	—	—	Nov. 26, 1881
Renselaer,	49	—	—	Mch. 26, 1876
Rathbun, Angelina A.,	41	6	—	Apr. 17, 1871
Amelia B.,	48	—	—	Jan. 13, 1888
Bessie,	17	—	—	May 7, 1896
Reeve, Samuel B.,	60	—	—	Oct. 6, 1866
Emily,	—	15	—	May 13, 1852
Mrs.,	—	—	—	Aug. 31, 1818
Reeves, Samuel,	68	—	—	Dec. 2, 1826
John,	81	—	—	Feb. 7, 1811
Enoch,	—	—	—	Jan. 6, 1837
Reynolds, Fanny H.,	32	—	—	Dec. 29, 1860
Rice, Mr.,	—	—	—	Sept. 14, 1803
Wm.,	—	—	—	Jan. 27, 1825
Richmond, Robert,	—	—	—	Apr. 29, 1886
Caroline,	—	—	—	July 18, 1882
Rogers, Sarah,	23	—	—	May 28, 1770
Roadley, Chas. H.,	—	—	12	Jan. 7, 1847
Robinson, David,	87	—	—	Mch. 15, 1806
Esther C.,	73	—	—	Apr. 10, 1803

Name of Deceased.	Age at Death.			Date of Death.
	Years.	Months.	Days.	
Robinson, John,	27	---	---	July 23, 1750
Rowley, Caroline A.,	3	---	---	Sept. 24, 1823
Frederic,	36		---	Nov. 5, 1861
Jane M.,	49		--	Aug. 15, 1866
Charlotte P.,	74	---	--	May 26, 1863
Asher N.,	78	---	---	Dec. 29, 1868
Dwight,	---	-	---	Feb. 16, 1875
Russell, John G.,	41	---	---	July 5, 1849
Abigail R.,	50	---	---	Nov. 19, 1865

Whole No. R's, 53.

S

	Years.	Months.	Days.	Date of Death.
Sage, Abner,	59	---	---	Mch. 24, 1818
Sally,	39	-	--	Feb. 6, 1802
Ruth,	29			Dec. 3, 1793
Edward C.,	7	--	1	Jan. 12, 1800
Almira,	44	---	--	June 8, 1835
Roderick,	42	--	-	July 29, 1825
Joseph,	64	--		May 23, 1812
Ruth,	44	-	--	Oct. 25, 1801
Ruth,	84		---	July 30, 1845
David,	29		---	
Sarah,	90	--	---	Feb. 10, 1817
David,	86	---		Nov. 25, 1803
Molley,	22	---	---	May 8, 1791
Henry,	17	---	---	Jan. 26, 1797
Honor,	53	---		Nov. 2, 1812
Elizabeth,	86	--	--	June 16, 1816
Betsey W.,	8		--	Jan. 6, 1814
David,	22	--	--	Oct. 16, 1798
Sybil,	73	---	---	Jan. 15, 1826
Enoch,	88	---	--	Mch. 9, 1840
Mary,	42			Oct. 9, 1832
Lucy,	75		--	Oct. 12, 1854
Hannah,	18		---	Sept. 4, 1767
Henry E.,	75	---	---	Aug. 14, 1872
Lucinda,	77	---	---	Oct. 22, 1875
Almira E.,	27	---		Aug. 28, 1859
Cornelius,	29	---	-	May 3, 1865
Edward,	49		--	May 3, 1865

Name of Deceased.	Age at Death.			Date of Death.
	Years.	Months.	Days.	
Sage, Henry,	65	—		Oct. 29, 1885
Chas. L.,	67	—		Aug. 9, 1864
Julia A.,	25	—	—	June 23, 1823
Frances,	39	—		May 14, 1844
Harriet W.,	59			May 12, 1884
Abner,	—	—	28	Mch. 10, 1835
Mary,		—	8	Aug. 28, 1836
Frances L.,	—	5	15	Nov. 13, 1820
Frances L.,	12	—		Aug. 7, 1837
Oliver P.,	27	—		Aug. 13, 1849
Philip,	69	—		June 8, 1855
Vienna,	91	5		Jan. 14, 1884
David,	87		—	1889
Ebenezer,		—	—	
Noah,		—	—	Sept 10, 1822
Jemima,	—	—	—	Nov. 14, 1884
Prudence,		—		
Walter,	—			Nov. 19, 1833
J.,	—	—	—	June 2, 1805
Savage, Catharine J.,	—	—	12	Mch. 30, 1835
Catharine J.,	—	—	3	Feb. 21, 1836
Anne,	36	—		Sept. 13, 1827
Luther,	57	—		Mch. 22, 1824
Scinthy,	—	5	—	Mch. 25, 1790
Caroline,	24	—	—	June 12, 1846
Desire,	26	—	—	July 11, 1828
Ira,	47	—	—	July 10, 1840
Nathaniel,	33	—	—	Nov. 26, 1769
Sarah,	9	—	—	July 17, 1890
Harriet,	59	—	—	Mch. 10, 1865
Prudence,	81	—	—	Oct 29, 1846
Harry B.,	2	2	—	Aug. 16, 1880
Caroline I.,	—	—	—	Apr. 10, 1854
Luther,	57	—	—	July 6, 1885
Nellie D.,	16	—	—	May 27, 1882
Saxton, George,	—	—	—	Apr. 29, 1813
Schellenx, Wm.,	57	—	—	Jan. 26, 1774
Mrs.,	—	—	—	Aug. 2, 1798
Abraham,	—,	—	—	Dec. 2, 1821
Schumacher, Carl G.,	50	—	—	Jan. 13, 1877
Edward L.,	14	—	—	Mch. 27, 1886
Sellew, Philip H.,	70	—	—	Jan. 18, 1873
Hannah,	30	—	—	Dec. 24, 1839
Theodosia A.,	84	—	—	Apr. 4, 1893

| Name of Deceased. | Age at Death. | | | Date of Death. |
	Years.	Months.	Days.	
Sellew, Philip,	26	10	28	Feb. 21, 1862
Hannah J.,	1	3	—	Jan. 1, 1841
Jane A.,	33	—	—	Feb. 2, 1891
Joseph,	50	—	—	Sept. 29, 1888
Shepard, Chas. G.,	4	7	—	Dec. 1, 1809
Lizzie A.,	3	9	—	July 7, 1859
Carrie E.,	12	3	—	Feb 7, 1870
Edward,	31	—	—	Jan. 16, 1848
Chauncey E.,	1	10	—	July 12, 1844
John,	68	—	—	Jan. 5, 1890
Sarah,	76	—	—	Oct. 21, 1888
Sarah E.,	44	—	—	July 18, 1855
Maria,	51	—	—	May 7, 1857
Eleanor,	74	—	—	May 8, 1856
Jonathan,	85	—	—	Mch. 15, 1867
David,	47	—	—	July 30, 1856
Noah,	67	6	—	Aug. 28, 1891
Eliza E.,	20	—	—	Feb. 24, 1844
Julia M.,	—	—	—	Aug. 18, 1896
John,	9	—	—	Nov. 3, 1803
Silence,	68	—	—	Jan. 28, 1792
Abigail,	17	—	—	Oct. 28, 1769
Bethiah,	—	—	—	
John,	73	—	—	Jan. 8, 1763
Elizabeth,	—	—	—	
Alden,	6	—	—	Nov. 24, 1813
Ansel P.,	4	—	—	Oct. 20, 1813
Elijah,	12	—	—	Aug. 28, 1823
Polly,	92	—	—	Jan. 5, 1879
Nancy,	75	—	—	July 20, 1861
Lamenta,	81	—	—	Jan. 18, 1842
Amos,	76	—	—	Dec. 23, 1835
Hannah,	27	—	—	Oct. 29, 1780
John,	68	—	—	Aug. 8, 1825
Elizabeth,	86	—	—	June 21, 1849
Mary A.,	2	10	—	Oct. 6, 1810
Daniel,	83	—	—	Oct. 19, 1866
Mary,	82	7	—	Dec. 11, 1867
Ruth,	87	—	—	Dec. 1, 1845
Phebe,	40	—	—	Dec. 19, 1796
Daniel,	97	—	—	Oct. 24, 1850
Reuben,	34	—	—	Nov. 16, 1794
Elizabeth,	5	—	—	Mch. 15, 1771
Nathaniel,	18	—	—	Oct. 25, 1794

Name of Deceased.	Years.	Months.	Days.	Date of Death.
Shepard, Sarah,	41	—	—	Jan. 10, 1773
Daniel,	76	—	—	Aug. 22, 1798
Grace,	83	—	—	Dec. 3, 1824
Sarah,	70	—	—	Jan. 14, 1826
George,	81	—	—	Jan. 25, 1844
Andrew,	63	—	—	June 3, 1830
Dilly,	37	—	—	Aug. 23, 1806
Dorinda N.,	88	—	—	Sept. 27, 1855
Noah,	71	—	—	Jan. 24, 1836
Ruth,	52	—	—	Nov. 18, 1821
Caroline,	18	—	—	Oct. 19, 1823
Caroline,	—	—	—	Apr. 1835
George,	34	—	—	Aug. 20, 1838
Lucy A.,	27	—	—	Aug. 5, 1838
Erastus	52	—	—	Sept. 15, 1843
Honor,	40	—	—	Mch. 23, 1832
Desire,	85	—	—	Jan. 30, 1878
Henry S.,	22	—	—	Jan. 8, 1856
Sophia,	—	—	—	Dec. 2, 1872
John,	73	—	—	Apr. 2, 1795
Grace,	—	—	—	Dec. 5, 1821
Shourt, Esther,	26	—	—	Mch. 3, 1784
Simpson, Amos,	57	—	—	Dec. 21, 1861
Ruth D.,	60	—	—	Aug. 2, 1864
Charley N.,	—	5	8	Sept. 1, 1885
Mrs. Harvey,	—	—	—	Apr. 19, 1882
Nelson C.,	1	6	—	Sept. 25, 1855
Smith, Henry R.,	57	—	—	July 23, 1875
Mary D.,	36	—	—	Jan. 22, 1854
Daniel,	62	—	—	Mch. 5, 1844
Jennet,	62	—	—	Nov. 9, 1843
Joel R.,	21	—	—	May 25, 1826
Joel,	37	—	—	Mch. 8, 1864
Steward, Bertie,	—	9	—	Mch. 6, 1873
Stewart, Chas.,	27	—	—	June 22, 1831
Betsey,	93	—	—	Oct. 13, 1873
Fanny,	79	—	—	Nov 5, 1865
Clarissa,	77	—	—	June 29, 1861
John,	55	—	—	Mch. 30, 1830
Daniel,	81	—	—	Apr. 28, 1826
Elizabeth,	76	—	—	Oct. 2, 1823
Michael,	74	—	—	Nov. 27, 1781
Samuel,	45	—	—	Apr. 27, 1817
Margaret,	57	—	—	June 12, 1770
Grace,	72	—	—	Aug. 26, 1838

Name of Deceased.	Age at Death.			Date of Death.
	Years.	Months.	Days.	
Stewart, Susanna,	—	—	16	Dec. 29, 1788
Daniel,	1	10	—	Nov. 9, 1777
Daniel,	—	2	—	Aug. 13, 1779
Elizabeth,	-	4	—	Oct. 12, 1779
Jane,	12	—	—	Mch. 2, 1767
James,	52	—	—	Apr. 13, 1822
Grace,	33	—	—	July 4, 1806
Eliza,	66	—	—	June 4, 1870
Delia,	6	1	—	Sept. 25, 1870
Mary J.,	42	—	—	Oct. 1, 1877
Emma F.,	52	—	—	Feb. 24, 1895
Emeline B.,	35	—	—	Aug. 13, 1868
Ralph H.,	—	3	12	Dec. 27, 1867
Ralph,	84	—	—	Nov. 7, 1886
Emeline,	85	-	—	Dec. 12, 1891
Sanford,	77	—	—	May 2, 1874
Sally,	62	—	—	Oct. 22, 1859
Thomas,	44	—	—	July 13, 1820
Sarah E.,	33	—	—	June 20, 1885
Delia A.,	19	—	—	Jan. 8, 1866
Hector,	68	—	—	Feb. 14, 1864
Aurelia,	59	—	—	May 4, 1862
Michael,	84	—	—	Jan. 18, 1844
Melinda,	50	—	—	Sept. 5, 1812
Catharine,	42	—	—	Oct. 16, 1827
Emeline B.,	6	3	—	Nov. 23, 1872
Stevens, Sara O.,	61	—	—	Mch. 13, 1897
Frederic M.,	48	—	—	Feb. 11, 1870
Isaac,	58	—	—	Feb. 25, 1848
Nabby B.,	81	6	—	Jan. 30, 1876
Norman B.,	—	—	—	July 24, 1894
Stevenson, John,	3	—	—	July 26, 1770
Joshua,	2	5	—	Sept. 17, 1771
Robert,	—	6	—	Dec. 26, 1768
Robert,	41	—	—	Feb. 8, 1777
Sarah,	44	—	—	Nov. 29, 1781
Stocking, Sylvester,	81	—	—	May 21, 1868
Martha B.,	94	—	—	Mch. 31, 1881
David S.,	72	—	—	June 12, 1884
Harriot,	19	—	—	Jan. 4, 1813
Phebe,	47	—	—	Nov. 23, 1784
Benjamin,	77	—	—	Dec. 4, 1808
Mrs. E.,	—	—	—	Oct. 10, 1803
John,	43	—	—	Oct. 12, 1854

Name of Deceased.	Age at Death.			Date of Death.
	Years.	Months.	Days.	
Stocking, Joseph A.,	46	—	—	June 5, 1881
Norman H.,	7	—	—	Apr. 16, 1883
Nellie E.,	8	—	—	Mch. 13, 1884
George,	42	—	—	Apr. 22, 1862
George,	—	5	11	Oct. 6, 1870
Olive,	75	—	—	Feb. 21, 1832
Eber,	73	—	—	Aug. 26, 1828
Stephen,	51	—	—	May 20, 1775
Mary,	92	—	—	Mch 9, 1825
Stephen,	—	—	—	Dec. 30, 1787
Elijah,	84	—	—	Nov. 4, 1852
Polly,	79	—	—	Sept. 29, 1852
Abiah,	63	—	—	Oct. 13, 1767
Samuel,	73	—	—	July 21, 1777
Hannan,	84	—	—	Dec. 1, 1817
Elijah,	79	—	—	July 18, 1807
Hannah,	26	—	—	Oct. 23, 1784
Mary,	—	—	—	Apr. 16, 1821
Strickland, Abel,	74	—	—	Mch. 2, 1823
Esther,	60	—	—	Apr. 8, 1815
Phebe,	56	—	—	Mch. 1, 1845
Joel,	4	—	—	May 12, 1788
Martha,	57	—	—	Nov. 22, 1774
Seth,	70	—	—	July 15, 1828
Anna,	94	—	—	May 16, 1856
Amy,	97	—	—	Sept. 4, 1897
Martha,	78	—	—	Apr. 15, 1876
Asenath,	94	8	—	Feb. 11, 1880
Vienna,	60	—	—	Dec. 26, 1863
Noah,	83	—	—	Apr. 14, 1859
Phebe C.,	74	—	—	July 4, 1865
Frederick A.,	33	—	—	Dec. 4, 1853
Silas B.,	50	—	—	May 7, 1856
Harriet R.,	75	—	—	Dec. 26, 1891
Noah,	30	—	—	Oct. 27, 1869
Butler,	17	—	—	
Noah J.,	9	—		
Noah N.,	76	8	—	Apr. 1, 1877
Caroline M.,	76	—	—	Mch. 28, 1883
Rhoda B.,	35	—	—	Jan. 20, 1870
Samuel,	—	—	—	Feb. 28, 1846
Joel,	78	—	—	July 27, 1864
Sarah L.,	85	—	—	Sept. 27, 1874
Alvin,	2	—	—	Aug. 31, 1815

Name of Deceased.	Age at Death.			Date of Death.
	Years.	Months.	Days.	
Strickland, Esther,	—	3	—	June 1, 1816
Chas.,	33	—	—	Nov. 15, 1850
Alanson,	80	—	—	July 31, 1888
Emily R.,	85	—	—	Feb. 10, 1894
William S.,	62	—	—	Oct. 30, 1889
Zerviah M.,	—	6	—	Aug. 26, 1850
George,	63	—	—	Aug. 11, 1878
Elizabeth A.,	59	—	—	Jan. 24, 1871
George E.,	2	—	—	Nov. 18, 1836
Elizabeth A.,	14	—	—	Feb. 17, 1854
Flora,	—	—	35	May 1, 1854
Abbie B.,	55	—	—	Sept. 10, 1895
Howard,	1	—	—	1871
Mabel,	1	—	—	1874
Freddie,	—	—	—	1879
Wm. K.,	29	—	—	1888
Asa,	79	—	—	Jan. 6, 1877
Nancy,	82	—	—	June 18, 1882
Thaddeus T.,	27	—	—	Mch. 18, 1855
Ammial,	55	—	—	Aug. 3, 1848
Susan A. P.,	84	—	—	Nov. 28, 1880
Lydia,	—	—	—	May 9, 1803
Mrs. N.,	—	—	—	July 8, 1808
Strong, Chas. W.,	—	14	—	Mch. 8, 1793
Anne,	5	—	—	Mch. 5, 1773
Florella,	6	—	—	May 14, 1775
Elnathan,	1	—	—	Nov. 9, 1784
Sarah,	38	—	—	Sept. 4, 1785
Abigail,	37	—	—	May 2, 1796
Cyprian, D. D.,	68	—	—	Nov. 17, 1811
Erastus,	82	—	—	Dec. 18, 1871
Mary L.,	76	—	—	May 12, 1875
Mary A.,	52	—	—	Sept. 20, 1874
Elizabeth,	3	—	—	July 23, 1863
Asaph,	65	8	—	Feb. 26, 1888
Baby,	—	—	—	
Julia A.,	2	—	—	Oct. 6, 1848
Helena,	5	—	—	Oct. 12, 1853
Joseph E.,	5	—	—	Oct. 7, 1861
Summers, Dudley C.,	82	—	—	June 20, 1851
Tabitha,	97	—	—	Apr. 3, 1873

Whole No. S's, 290.

T

Name of Deceased.	Age at Death.			Date of Death.
	Years.	Months.	Days.	
Tallcott, Rev. Hervey.	75	—	—	Dec. 19, 1865
Cynthia,	69	—	—	Apr. 23, 1869
Maria,	17	—	—	June 27, 1848
Taylor, Ellen,	—	—	9	May 4, 1849
Myra M.,	—	—	—	
Mary,	84	10	—	Oct. 7, 1892
Chauncy,	51	—	—	May 11, 1854
Annie R.,	—	—	—	
Jane,	—	—	—	June 22, 1892
Henry W.,	—	—	—	May 17, 1889
Gurdon,	80	6	—	Jan. 30, 1870
Ruth M.,	78	—	—	May 10, 1885
Marid,	—	—	10	July 3, 1833
Fanny,	—	21	11	Nov. 3, 1838
Teller, Agnes A.,	—	6	21	Aug. 5, 1881
Thompson, Margaret,	82	—	—	Dec. 3, 1834
Thomas, John H.,	44	—	—	Feb. 28, 1865
Eliza,	75	—	—	Aug. 15, 1896
Tilden, Ada E.,	3	1	—	Jan. 30, 1881
Susie E.,	2	7	—	May 2, 1885
Tory, Lydia,	—	—	—	Mch. 1, 1834
Tousler, Mrs. E.,	—	—	—	May 13, 1829
Treat, Talatha (Sexton),	75	2	6	Apr. 18, 1858
Tryon, David,	—	—	—	Apr. 25, 1808
Mary A.,	—	—	—	Mch. 30, 1828
Turner, Betsey,	2	8	—	Nov. 24, 1827
Roswell,	4	—	—	Nov. 24, 1827
Asahel,	—	—	10	June 13, 1821
Roswell,	4	—	—	Mch. 30, 1831
Mrs. R.,	—	—	—	Aug. 10, 1832
Betsey,	—	—	—	July 7, 1821
Tyler, Richard,	—	3	5	Feb. 16, 1835

Whole No. T's, 32.

U

Ufford, Sarah,	92	—	—	Feb. 10, 1851
Adeliza,	2	—	—	Jan. 7, 1843
Charity P.,	86	—	—	Jan. 9, 1894

Name of Deceased.	Age at Death.			Date of Death.
	Years.	Months	Days.	
Ufford, Patience,	1	—	—	Feb. 29, 1774
Geo. H.,	35	—	—	July 30, 1861
Russell,	67	—	—	Nov. 11, 1869
John,	—	—	—	Aug. 21, 1798
Mrs. J.,	—	—	—	Jan. 9, 1819

Whole No. U's, 8.

V

Valentine, Henry,	21	—	—	Sept. 11, 1853
Lucy,	1	—	2	Sept. 2, 1854
Chauncy,	57	.	—	Apr. 18, 1852
Abigail,	43	—	—	Oct. 18, 1856
Van Veghten, H. W.,	67	—	—	May 19, 1882
Vary, Mrs. J.,	—	. .		Oct. 2, 1830
Ventres, Alexander,	—	—		Dec. 26, 1856

Whole No. V's, 7.

W

Wadsworth, Honnor,	56	—	—	Jan. 31, 1789
Waldo, Lucius,	—	—	—	Oct. 22, 1881
Cora A.,	—	13		May 10, 1864
Ward, Wm.,	38	—	—	Mch. 3, 1848
Wm. E.,	22	—	—	Aug. 13, 1831
Warner, Lucy,	—	—	—	Dec. 20, 1804
Deliverance,	—	—	—	May 22, 1813
Orrin,	47	—		Mch. 3, 1897
Orrin,	—	—	—	
Washburn, John,	4	—	—	Sept. 17, 1797
Welles, Thomas,	40	—	—	Feb. 23, 1792
Joseph,	43	—	—	Apr. 18, 1823
Clarissa,	34	—	—	Dec. 18, 1824
Rebecca,	35	—	—	Aug. 6, 1814
Eunice,	18	—	—	Dec. 11, 1823
Wells, Mabel,	89	—	—	June 29, 1824
Jessie,	6	—	—	1870
Henry H.,	71	—	—	Aug. 27, 1892
Anna,	77	—	—	Dec. 14, 1876

Name of Deceased.	Years.	Months.	Days.	Date of Death.
Weils, Roswell,	82	—	—	Apr. 20, 1876
Celestia M.,	28	—		Aug. 29, 1861
Almira,	22	—		Jan. 26, 1819
Nancy,	72	—		May 21, 1839
Mary L.,	67	8		Sept. 21, 1897
West, Brackett,	58	—		Oct. 18, 1866
Mary Ann,	72			Sept. 6, 1885
B. Revilo,	64	—	—	Nov. 15, 1897
Wetherell, Jonathan,	88		—	Aug. 29, 1895
Mary A.,	60		—	Feb. 11, 1875
Wheeler, Wm.,	55		—	Mch. 29, 1872
Edward,	64	—	—	Oct. 13, 1841
Elizabeth,	71	—	—	Sept. 2, 1850
Chas. W.,	78	—	—	Aug. 30, 1881
Laura,	84	—	—	Mch. 18, 1895
White, Ebenezer B.,	56	—	—	Jan. 12, 1861
Maria,	15	—	—	Sept. 13, 1845
Daniel,	80	—	—	Dec. 25, 1845
Abigail,	65	—	—	Feb. 22, 1838
Chas. H.,	3	4	—	Mch. 20, 1866
Almira W.,	33	—	—	Dec. 11, 1866
Sarah M.,	—	—	—	Oct. 14, 1846
James W.,	68	—	—	Jan. 9, 1870
Fanny H.,	20		—	Nov. 8, 1825
Margaret B.,	86	—	—	July 10, 1888
Wm. S.,	70	—	—	Jan. 12, 1895
Emily S.,	58	—	—	June 14, 1883
Stephen H.,	74	—	—	Oct. 10, 1894
Stephen,	44	—	—	Nov. 23, 1774
Anne,	10	—	—	May 2, 1775
Mollie,	8	—	—	May 27, 1777
Ebenezer,	90	—	—	July 27, 1817
Ruth,	53	—	—	Nov. 23, 1780
Esther,	82	—	—	July 14, 1845
Mary,	79	—	—	Dec. 15, 1838
David,	79	—	—	Sept. 18, 1833
Mary Ann,	46	—	—	Dec. 4, 1797
Mary Ann,	12	—	—	Nov. 6, 1810
Amos,	—	—	21	Feb. 8, 1774
Nathaniel,	52	—	—	Feb. 11, 1767
Mary,	51	—	—	Jan. 31, 1767
Lois,	71	—	—	Aug. 31, 1795
Noadiah,	5	—	—	Dec. 16, 1776
Evelyn,	80	—	—	Oct. 16, 1886
Ward,	15	—	—	Sept. 13, 1847

Name of Deceased.	Years.	Months.	Days.	Date of Death.
White, Frances E. P.,	83	—	—	Mch. 8, 1892
Abigail,	59	—	—	
Mary,	53	—	—	Nov. 9, 1705
Joseph,	—	—	—	1770
Mehetabel,	22	—	—	Mch. 15, 1745
Nathaniel,	59	—	—	May 5, 1743
David,	57	—	—	Oct. 27, 1836
Abigail,	60	—	—	Dec. 19, 1839
Maria,	75	—	—	July 22, 1879
Hannah,	77	—	—	Feb. 23, 1863
George,	85	—	—	June 1, 1848
Mabel,	51	—	—	Dec. 6, 1817
Hannah,	32	—	—	Sept. 21, 1792
Mehetabel,	—	—	—	1744
Abigail,	3	—	—	Oct. 20, 1759
John,	—	—	—	May 20, 1825
Earle E.,	2	6	10	Nov. 13, 1858
Whiting, Isaac,	—	—	—	Apr. 26, 1828
Whitmore, Demas S.,	35	—	—	Feb. 28, 1849
Marionette P.,	29	—	—	Feb. 28, 1849
Daniel,	27	—	—	Dec. 23, 1798
Wilcox, Aaron,	—	—	—	Mch. 8, 1820
Sarah,	—	—	—	May 18, 1816
Elizabeth N.,	90	—	—	July, 1860
Horace B.,	66	9	—	Apr. 5, 1888
Wm. B.,	19	—	—	Sept. 16, 1868
Luther,	84	—	—	Mch. 12, 1864
Lucy B.,	67	—	—	Feb. 2, 1855
Lucy C.,	39	—	—	Aug. 25, 1811
Sarah,	40	—	—	Jan. 13, 1818
Aaron, Jr.,	33	—	—	May 1, 1808
Sarah,	74	—	—	Mch. 6, 1820
Aaron,	68	—	—	Oct. 18, 1813
Lucy,	39	—	—	Oct. 25, 1811
Asahel,	46	—	—	Oct. 31, 1817
Mary P. R.,	22	—	—	Nov. 4, 1826
Wm. W.,	22	—	—	Nov. 6, 1824
Caroline,	40	—	—	Sept. 18, 1868
Willcox, Lucy,	21	—	—	Jan. 8, 1802
Williams, Betsey,	8	—	—	Sept. 16, 1795
Lois,	63	—	—	Dec. 21, 1830
David,	73	—	—	Aug. 12, 1863
Laura,	40	—	—	Oct. 8, 1828
Sally C.,	83	—	—	July 18, 1888

Name of Deceased	Age at Death.			Date of Death.
	Years.	Months.	Days.	
Williams, Chas.,	10	—	—	Oct. 10, 1830
Mary,	1		—	Mch. 7, 1827
Martha,	3	—	—	Oct. 20, 1829
William,	72	—	—	Jan. 3, 1835
William,	—			Dec. 22, 1830
James,	—		—	Sept. 3, 1827
Wilson, William,	54	—		July 19, 1882
Winters, Mrs.,	—	—	—	Sept. 15, 1883
Wolcott, James M.,	45	—	—	Sept. 12, 1878
Wood, Jabez,	—	—		Sept. 20, 1812
Worterman, Mercy,	—	—	—	June 12, 1815
* Welles,				
Helen (Penfield),	42	—	—	May 23, 1866

Whole No. W's, 120.

Y

Yongs, Daniel,	—	—	—	Dec. 18, 1799

Whole No. Y's, 1.

Grand Total, 1568.

* This name appears on Capt. Russell Penfield's monument, but the remains are buried in Cedar Hill Cemetery, Hartford, Conn.

ERRATA.

Page 37. Robert Akins died Oct. 27, 1795. Roard Akins was buried Oct. 27, 1795. The former was taken from grave stone; the latter from sexton's record of Seth Strickland. They may be one and the same person.

Page 44. Alfred H. Conklin is spelled as the name is cut on grave stone. This may have been a mistake in the inscription, as this family always spelled the name "Concklin."

Page 67. Dilly Shepard was Deliverance Leland Shepard, Dilly being the abbreviation as cut on the gravestone.

In a few cases where the date of *death* could not be obtained from records or inscriptions, the date of *burial* has been taken from the records of sextons and put in the foregoing list under the heading of date of death.

ADDENDA.

There were eight (8) burials in 1897, by John Strickland, Sexton, after the list on page 32 was printed. This makes the total number nineteen (19), for the year 1897.

Since the History of the Cemetery was put in type, the First Ecclesiastical Society of Portland has given the Association a quitclaim deed of their interest in the older part of the cemetery. This is the portion that was sold for burial purposes by William Bartlit, in A. D. 1767, and leased to the Burying Ground Association by the Ecclesiastical Society in A. D. 1862.

This deed is signed by Archibald C. Goodrich, Frederick W. Goodrich, and Ellery B. Taylor, the Society's Committee, duly authorized by a vote of the Society at its meeting held December 4, A. D. 1897. It is dated Jan. 3, A. D. 1898, and is recorded in the land records of the town of Portland, in Volume XVI., page 257. This deed completes the title of the Association to the entire cemetery.

By an instrument in writing dated July 7, A. D. 1897, the heirs and representatives of the founders and builders of the church edifice known as the Center Congregational Church granted to this Association the unlimited use of the church building and all its appurtenances, with the land, sheds and all other buildings thereon, for religious and funeral purposes. This grant is recorded in Vol. XVII., pages 397 and 398, of the Portland Land Records.

At a fair and supper given by the ladies in the basement of this church, on the afternoon and evening of October 12, A. D. 1897, and by contributions, the sum of $205.95 was raised. This, with voluntary labor, was applied towards the expense of putting the church building and sheds in good condition, also for building a retaining stone wall on the front and part of the west side of the church, with convenient steps, and the construction of a receiving vault in the basement. This provides the Association with a convenient and complete mortuary chapel.

By means of the permits now adopted by this Association a complete and permanent record is kept of all interments and disinterments in our cemetery, and the manner of giving deeds of lots is so devised that a detailed record of their ownership is secured.

The managers for themselves and for all the many friends of the Association desire to express and put upon record their appreciation of the efficient and disinterested services of the Superintendent, Mr. Henry Kilby, and others in successfully accomplishing these recent improvements. Also to thank the ladies for their generous aid.

The attention of all persons having friends interred in this cemetery is called to the importance of having inscribed grave marks at the graves. They not only mark the place where our friends rest but the inscription is a permanent record of their birth and death.

While there may be good reasons why grave stones have not been placed in individual cases the number of unmarked graves in our cemetery is a cause of deep regret. That our dead may not appear to be forgotten the managers earnestly request that this matter receive careful consideration and attention.

* 9 7 8 3 3 3 7 1 9 1 6 3 4 *